QUICK

COMPREHENSIVE

EASY-T

THE ACAD...   ...OK HAS IT

**Nomina...   ...tegory from 1927 to the
...ent

** ...on, who lost and why

**Inside gossip

**Hints on how to choose the winners

**A complete index of films and actors

AND DOZENS OF EXCITING PHOTOS OF YOUR
FAVORITE STARS!

BOOK YOUR PLACE ON OUR WEBSITE AND MAKE THE READING CONNECTION!

We've created a customized website just for our very special readers, where you can get the inside scoop on everything that's going on with Zebra, Pinnacle and Kensington books.

When you come online, you'll have the exciting opportunity to:

- View covers of upcoming books
- Read sample chapters
- Learn about our future publishing schedule (listed by publication month *and author*)
- Find out when your favorite authors will be visiting a city near you
- Search for and order backlist books from our online catalog
- Check out author bios and background information
- Send e-mail to your favorite authors
- Meet the Kensington staff online
- Join us in weekly chats with authors, readers and other guests
- Get writing guidelines
- AND MUCH MORE!

Visit our website at
http://www.pinnaclebooks.com

THE ACADEMY AWARDS® HANDBOOK

REVISED AND UPDATED 2000 EDITION

JOHN HARKNESS

P

PINNACLE BOOKS

KENSINGTON PUBLISHING CORP.

http://www.pinnaclebooks.com

ACKNOWLEDGEMENTS

I'd like to acknowledge a number of friends who, for reasons known only to themselves, collect the Academy Awards® on videotape, and were kind enough to loan them to me. Also, the microfilm and periodicals staff at the Metro Toronto Reference Library, who kept me supplied with old issues of *Variety*. I'd also like to thank my agent, Scott Siegel, and my editor, Paul Dinas, who left me alone as I missed deadline after deadline during the writing of this book.

INTRODUCTION:
THE ENVELOPE, PLEASE . . .

The Academy Awards® exist to honor and promote Hollywood's own creations. We have, year after year, heard that the Best Picture Oscar® will add X–million dollars to a film's grosses. The public, I suspect, sees the Oscars® in a different way. For us, the Academy Awards® are a storehouse of memories, of moments and lines, of emotional highs and embarrassing lows.

We remember the flabberghasted look on Goldie Hawn's face when she opened the best actor envelope in 1970, Jonathan Demme's incoherent acceptance speech in 1991, Shirley Mac-Laine's "I deserve this" speech in 1983 and Sally Field's "you like me" speech in 1984 . . .

Yet the Academy also remembers for us. I "remember" seeing things on the Oscars® that I am too young to remember seeing, because the Oscar® show has become a kind of video mausoleum. Are our memories live or are they acquired courtesy of videotape? Is that question finally important? Doing the research for this book, I was shocked to find that the Charlie Chaplin Honorary Oscar® was all the way back in 1971—the event took place more than two decades ago, but I know I've seen it more recently than that.

The Academy of Motion Pictures Arts and Sciences were created in 1927 as a kind of "super union," and only the elite of the industry were invited to join. The various crafts groups, especially the directors, writers and actors, soon found that an organization dominated by producers was not going to do the aforementioned groups any favors whatsoever, and began forming their own guilds.

The Academy Awards® were an afterthought, but have since become the tail that wags the dog. The function of the AMPAS, in the public mind, is to create the awards show which startles and appals us with equal regularity. What makes an Academy Award®–winning film is open to debate. After all, they went almost sixty years after *Cimarron* without naming another Western as Best Picture, then they name two Westerns in three years, in an era when the Western is supposed to be dead. Oscar®–winning pictures have often been great and static adventures in what we might call official middlebrow liberal culture. But, as non–winner Martin Scorsese has noted, "They don't give them out lightly. After all, John Ford won six of them." But Alfred Hitchcock, like Scorsese, never won any of them. The Academy has an appalling fondness for one shots, oddities, and bizarre casting, yet are capable of rising up and honoring some people at exactly the right moment for exactly the right film.

The Academy Awards® as we know them began in 1952, the first time the Awards were telecast nationally. Once, the Oscars® were the only place to see clips from the year's best films—my family decided to see *Butch Cassidy and the Sundance Kid* based on the clips at the Oscars®—now half the shows on television seem to run clips. Once, the Oscars® were the only place to see famous and talented people making fools of themselves, now there's "Oprah" and "Sally Jesse Raphael." But they still hold our attention. In a graceless and inelegant age, they offer the dream of glamor.

The book is organized on a year–by–year basis, with the years occasionally augmented by lists of interesting trivia. Some of the awards have shifted around during the years. Art Direction, for example, was initially Interior Decoration, then Art Direction—Set Decoration. I have referred to it throughout as Art Direction. What we call Screenplay and Adapted Screenplay actually have much longer names, but I have chosen to go with the popular shorthand, for consistency. What we now call Honorary Oscars® were initially Special Oscars®.

The comments at the end of each year's section follow no set pattern. I began working anecdotally, but too many of the good anecdotes have been repeated too often. Working through the years, strange connections began to form, odd observations, and a realization that while we sit through the Irving Thalberg Award and the Jean Hersholt Award and listen to jokes about Jack Valenti's speaking style, nobody ever explains exactly who these people are. In the short space permitted, I have treated each year as it struck me to treat it.

It struck me as pointless to start second–guessing the Awards

8

(I do it occasionally, but not often) simply because the Oscar®– winners in any given years are not godlike electees whose names and deeds belong to the ages. The Academy Awards® work on an alarmingly ad hoc basis, and this year's immortal treasure is next year's regrettable error. So a group of supposedly sane people in 1937 decided that "Sweet Leilani," from that long forgotten non– classic *Waikiki Wedding* was a better song than George and Ira Gershwin's "They Can't Take That Away From Me." So what? One should treat each year's awards less as nominees for the hall of fame than as a snapshot of that year, a moment that frames what Hollywood thought was its best at that time, where its sentimental attachments lay. Look at the nominees in the late '60s and early '70s, when *Anne of the Thousand Days* competed with *Patton*. Does anyone think Don Ameche's Oscar® was actually for his performance in *Cocoon?*

The last chapter provides you with my system for winning your office pool—you can, with a little luck, recoup the cost of this book. In the past twelve years, I have won my own office pool outright twice and tied three times. I developed my system over the years, codifying it before the 1992 Oscars®. Shortly thereafter, I went on television (CBC Newsworld in Canada) and predicted Marisa Tomei's "completely unexpected" victory as best supporting actress. In 1992, the system gave me fifteen of the 22 winners, and only a sentimental attachment to Susan Sarandon prevented a sweep of the major categories.

1927—28

Best Production (two winners)	*The Last Command* The Racket Seventh Heaven The Way of All Flesh * Wings
Artistic Quality of Production	Chang The Crowd * Sunrise
Actor	Richard Barthelmess, *The Noose, The Patent Leather Kid* Charles Chaplin, *The Circus* *Emil Jannings, *The Last Command, The Way Of All Flesh*
Actress	Louise Dresser, *A Ship Comes In* *Janet Gaynor, *Seventh Heaven, Street Angel, Sunrise* Gloria Swanson, *Sadie Thompson*
Director	*Frank Borzage, *Seventh Heaven* Herbert Brenon, *Sorrell and Son* King Vidor, *The Crowd*
Comedy Direction	Charles Chaplin, *The Circus* * Lewis Milestone, *Two Arabian Knights* Ted Wilde, *Speedy*

Writing: (Adaptation) Benjamin Glazer, *Seventh Heaven*
(Original Story) Ben Hecht, *Underworld*
(Titles) Joseph Farnham, *Telling the World*

Cinematography: Charles Rosher and Karl Struss, *Sunrise*

Art Direction: William Cameron Menzies, *The Dove, The Tempest*

Engineering Effects: Roy Pomeroy, *Wings*

Honorary Oscars®: Warner Brothers, for *The Jazz Singer*.
Charles Chaplin, for writing, acting, directing, and producing *The Circus*.

The more things change, the more they remain the same. The first Oscars® featured controversial decisions, sops thrown to the los-

*Denotes winner.

Left: Charlie Chaplin, winner of the first Honorary Oscar®, for *The Circus. Right:* Janet Gaynor, Best Actress winner for *Seventh Heaven,* with co-star Charles Farrell.

ers, and complaints from the winners. At the early awards, the Academy membership voted for nominees, and Academy's Board of Governors decided the winners.

The Board decided that it was unfair for the last silent films to compete with *The Jazz Singer*, so they ruled it ineligible and gave it a special award. The Board wanted to give the award for Artistic Production to *The Crowd*, but Louis B. Mayer came to the meeting and argued—exhaustingly—that the award should go to F. W. Murnau's *Sunrise*. He was right, though both *The Crowd* and *Sunrise* are great films, but for the wrong reasons. Mayer's argument was that on the one hand, *The Crowd* had a horrible message (a man could work hard and achieve insignificance) and on the other, Murnau was a great international filmmaker, and if the Academy honored him, some of his prestige would rub off.

Despite the three–month period between the announcement of the winners and the awards banquet, Best Actor Emil Jannings missed the dinner (he sent a telegram) and so did Best Original Story winner Ben Hecht, who complained that Josef Von Sternberg had ruined the script to *Underworld*. And at the Awards dinner itself, Al Jolson began the long tradition of mocking the awards: "I notice they gave *The Jazz Singer* a statuette, but they didn't give me one. I could use one. They look heavy and I need another paperweight."

13

1928–29

Production	Alibi
	* Broadway Melody
	Hollywood Revue
	In Old Arizona
	The Patriot

Actor	George Bancroft, Thunderbolt
	* Warner Baxter, In Old Arizona
	Chester Morris, Alibi
	Paul Muni, The Valiant
	Lewis Stone, The Patriot

Actress	Ruth Chatterton, Madam X
	Betty Compson, The Barker
	Jeanne Eagels, The Letter
	Bessie Love, Broadway Melody
	* Mary Pickford, Coquette

Director	Lionel Barrymore, Madame X
	Harry Beaumont, Broadway Melody
	Irving Cummings, In Old Arizona
	* Frank Lloyd, The Divine Lady, Weary River, Drag
	Ernst Lubitsch, The Patriot

Writing: Hans Kraly, *The Patriot*

Cinematography: Clyde DeVinna, *White Shadows in the South Seas*

Art Direction: Cedric Gibbons, *The Bridge at San Luis Rey*

Rule Changes: Artistic Quality of Production, Comedy Direction, Title Writing, Engineering Effects Awards discarded.

Deciding that the best way to attract stars and attention to the Awards was not to name the winners until the awards banquet, The Academy began to create the Awards show as we know it. This year, however, the judges took almost six months to decide who were the winners—the Awards were not given out until April 30, 1930—when several of the films nominated had premiered in August of 1928.

When the awards were finally handed out, the Academy faced charges that it was evolving less into an industry organization than a small club devoted to the promotion of its founders. Char-

Above: Mary Pickford, Best Actress winner for *Coquette. Right:* Anita Page, star of the Best Picture of 1928–29, *Broadway Melody.*

ter members of the Academy dominated the awards and nominations—director Frank Lloyd, art director and statuette creator Cedric Gibbons, and Mary Pickford, wife of first president Fairbanks, whose Best Actress prize for *Coquette* raised eyebrows all over Hollywood.

When the 1929–1930 Awards were given, less than six months later, they were decided by a vote of the full Academy membership, though even this process was not felt to be incorruptible.

1929—30

Production	*_All Quiet on the Western Front_
	The Big House
	Disraeli
	The Divorcee
	The Love Parade

Director	Clarence Brown, _Anna Christie_
	Clarence Brown, _Romance_
	Robert Z. Leonard, _The Divorcee_
	Ernst Lubitsch, _The Love Parade_
	*Lewis Milestone, _All Quiet on the Western Front_
	King Vidor, _Hallelujah_

Actor	*George Arliss, _Disraeli_
	George Arliss, _The Green Goddess_
	Wallace Beery, _The Big House_
	Maurice Chevalier, _The Love Parade_
	Maurice Chevalier, _The Big Pond_
	Ronald Colman, _Bulldog Drummond_
	Ronald Colman, _Condemned_
	Lawrence Tibbett, _The Rogue Song_

Actress	Nancy Carroll, _The Devil's Holiday_
	Ruth Chatterton, _Sarah and Son_
	Greta Garbo, _Anna Christie_
	Greta Garbo, _Romance_
	*Norma Shearer, _The Divorcee_
	Norma Shearer, _Their Own Desire_
	Gloria Swanson, _The Trespasser_

Writing: Frances Marion, _The Big House_

Cinematography: Joseph T. Rucker, Willard Van Der Veer, _With Byrd at the South Pole_

Art Direction: Herman Rosse, _The King of Jazz_

Sound: Douglas Shearer, _The Big House_

Rule Changes: Sound Recording added as a category. All members of the Academy vote on the final ballot.

If you were transported back to the Awards ceremonies of the '30s, you would not recognize them. The 1929–30 Awards were

Left: Oscar® winner for Best Picture, *All Quiet on the Western Front. Right:* Norma Shearer, Best Actress for *The Divorcee.*

held in a ballroom at the Ambassador Hotel, and the dinner and dancing came first. After that, the evening began with a lengthy speech from Will Hays, the head of Hollywood's self–censorship. After the Academy's financial report, they began giving out the awards.

They also did not build to Best Picture the way they do today—they gave director first, sound recording and interior decoration second, cinematography and writing, then best picture, followed by the acting awards. The most interesting sidelight to the Oscars® was that the winners were supposed to be secret, but acting winners George Arliss and Norma Shearer both posed with the statuettes two days before the awards show.

The Oscars® for best actress Norma Shearer and sound engineer Douglas Shearer marked the first instance of blood relatives winning Oscars®. Six decades later, not even their highly unusual feat of winning them in the same year is unique—the Hustons matched it in 1948, the Coppolas in 1974.

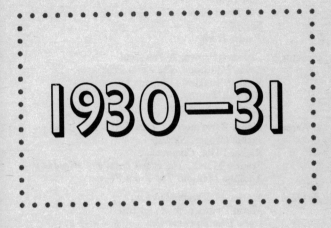

Picture	*Cimmaron
	East Lynne
	The Front Page
	Skippy
	Trader Horn

Director	Clarence Brown, *A Free Soul*
	Lewis Milestone, *The Front Page*
	Wesley Ruggles, *Cimarron*
	*Norman Taurog, *Skippy*
	Josef Von Sternberg, *Morocco*

Actor	*Lionel Barrymore, *A Free Soul*
	Jackie Cooper, *Skippy*
	Richard Dix, *Cimarron*
	Fredric March, *The Royal Family of Broadway*
	Adolphe Menjou, *The Front Page*

Actress	Marlene Dietrich, *Morocco*
	*Marie Dressler, *Min and Bill*
	Irene Dunne, *Cimarron*
	Ann Harding, *Holiday*
	Norma Shearer, *A Free Soul*

Original Screenplay: John Monk Saunders, *The Dawn Patrol*

Adapted Screenplay: Howard Estabrook, *Cimarron*

Cinematography: Floyd Crosby, *Tabu*

Art Direction: Max Ree, *Cimarron*

Sound: Paramount Sound Department

Rule Changes: Best Production becomes Best Picture. The Writing Oscar® splits back into two awards, for adaptation and original script. The sound award goes to the work of a department rather than an individual or an individual film. The Sound Committee nominates, the membership votes, though what they would base the vote on is an odd thing to think about.

To be a good director, one needs a certain psychological insight. To be the Best Director, however, one needs a streak of brutality. Norman Taurog was directing his nephew, Jackie Cooper, in a film called *Skippy*. Having trouble getting the proper emotional response, he told the ten–year–old that if he didn't cry, the direc-

Left: Marie Dressler, Best Actress winner for *Min and Bill,* with Harpo Marx. *Right:* Lionel Barrymore, Best Actor for *A Free Soul.*

tor would shoot his dog. The picture was a big hit, the young actor got a nomination and the director got the statuette.

Cimarron—the only Western to win Best Picture until *Dances With Wolves* 60 years later—wins three Oscars®, and director Wesley Ruggles complains that he didn't win. Bruce Beresford, Barbra Streisand, Steven Spielberg are part of a long tradition.

Odd career ends for Oscar® winners, 1: Floyd Crosby, cinematographer of *Tabu*, spent the '60s shooting Roger Corman horror movies like *The Pit and the Pendulum.*

Picture   *Arrowsmith*
               Bad Girl
               The Champ
               Five Star Final
             * *Grand Hotel*
               Shanghai Express
               The Smiling Lieutenant

Director   *Frank Borzage, *Bad Girl*
              King Vidor, *The Champ*
              Josef Von Sternberg, *Shanghai Express*

Actor   *Wallace Beery, *The Champ*
(two winners) Alfred Lunt, *The Guardsman*
             * Fredric March, *Dr. Jekyll and Mr. Hyde*

Actress   Marie Dressler, *Emma*
             Lynn Fontanne, *The Guardsman*
           * Helen Hayes, *The Sin of Madelon Claudet*

Original Screenplay: Frances Marion, *The Champ*

Adapted Screenplay: Edwin Burke, *Bad Girl*

Cinematography: Lee Garmes, *Shanghai Express*

Art Direction: Gordon Wiles, *Transatlantic*

Sound: Paramount Sound Department

Short subjects: (cartoon) "Flowers and Trees" (Disney)
     (comedy) "The Music Box" (Laurel and Hardy)
     (novelty) "Wrestling Swordfish"

Honorary Oscar®: Walt Disney for the creation of Mickey
     Mouse.

Rule Changes: Three Short Subject categories added. Only films
shot in America eligible for cinematography, no doubt in response
to the de facto conversion of Cinematography into a "best use of
exotic locales" in the previous years.

Nothing could more thoroughly indicate the difference between
today's Hollywood and '30s Hollywood than the introduction of
the awards for short films at the 1931–32 Awards. Now, short
films are an afterthought, with animation winners with unpronounceable names emerging from all corners of the globe.

Left: Greta Garbo, star of 1931–32 Best Picture, *Grand Hotel. Right:* Laurel & Hardy, stars of the Best Short Subject, "The Music Box."

Then, short films were an integral part of the movie–going process, and the presence of a new Mickey Mouse cartoon or Laurel and Hardy short was a powerful inducement on the marquee. Disney and Laurel and Hardy each received Oscars®, and Disney received a special award for the creation of Mickey Mouse.

For the first time, the Academy Awards® were broadcast nationally on radio. So they decided that there would be no speeches. Of course, there were—Lionel Barrymore, for example, gave a speech on the integrity of the awards.

On the other hand, they were counting the votes during the awards ceremony, and some time after Fredric March had been handed his statuette for *Dr. Jeckyll and Mr. Hyde,* it was discovered that he had beaten Wallace Beery by one vote—under Academy rules, three votes or less counted as a tie, so Wallace Beery received his award after Louis B. Mayer had picked up his for Best Picture.

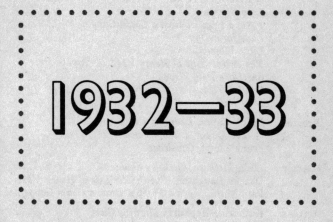

Picture	*Cavalcade
	A Farewell to Arms
	42nd Street
	I Am a Fugitive from a Chain Gang
	Lady for a Day
	Little Women
	The Private Life of Henry VIII
	She Done Him Wrong
	Smilin' Thru
	State Fair
Director	Frank Capra, Lady for a Day
	George Cukor, Little Women
	*Frank Lloyd, Cavalcade
Actor	Leslie Howard, Berkeley Square
	*Charles Laughton, The Private Life of Henry VIII
	Paul Muni, I Am a Fugitive From a Chain Gang
Actress	*Katharine Hepburn, Morning Glory
	May Robson, Lady For a Day
	Diana Wynyard, Cavalcade

Original Screenplay: Victor Heerman and Sarah Y. Mason, Little Women

Adapted Screenplay: Robert Lord, One Way Passage

Cinematography: Charles Bryant Lang, Jr., A Farewell to Arms

Art Direction: William S. Darling, Cavalcade

Sound: Harold C. Lewis, A Farewell To Arms

Short subjects: (cartoon) "Three Little Pigs" (Disney)
(comedy) "So This Is Harris"
(novelty) "Krakatoa"

Rule Changes: Assistant directors honored for the first time. Art Direction awards newly limited to American films.

In the midst of the depression, the Academy's biggest controversy had to do with economics rather than aesthetics. The Academy proposed an across the board pay cut of 50% for all studio employees to last two months. The writers resigned from the Acad-

Left: Katharine Hepburn, Best Actress, *Morning Glory. Right:* Charles Laughton, Best Actor for *The Private Life of Henry VIII.*

emy in protest and formed the Screenwriters' Guild. The Academy then proposed a new code that would cap the salaries of writers, actors and directors. This led to a mass exodus from the Academy and the formation of the Screen Actors' Guild. (Extensive accounts of this are available in *The Hollywood Writer Wars,* by Nancy Schwarz, and in Oscar®–winner Budd Schulberg's classic Hollywood novel, *What Makes Sammy Run?*)

One of the most embarrassing moments in the history of the Awards occurred when master of ceremonies Will Rogers opened the envelope containing the name of the best director and said "Come and get it, Frank!" without specifying which of the two nominated Franks (Capra and Lloyd) had won. Frank Capra was halfway to the podium when Rogers clarified that Frank Lloyd had won for *Cavalcade.* The winners of the acting prizes, however, felt that the best way to avoid embarrassment was to stay away— Katharine Hepburn was working on Broadway and Charles Laughton was in England.

1934

Picture	*The Barretts of Wimpole Street*
	Cleopatra
	Flirtation Walk
	The Gay Divorcee
	Here Comes the Navy
	The House of Rothschild
	Imitation of Life
	* It Happened One Night
	One Night of Love
	The Thin Man
	Viva Villa
	The White Parade
Director	*Frank Capra, *It Happened One Night*
	Victor Schertzinger, *One Night of Love*
	W.S. Van Dyke, *The Thin Man*
Actor	*Clark Gable, *It Happened One Night*
	Frank Morgan, *The Affairs of Cellini*
	William Powell, *The Thin Man*
Actress	*Claudette Colbert, *It Happened One Night*
	Grace Moore, *One Night of Love*
	Norma Shearer, *The Barretts of Wimpole Street*

Original Screenplay: Arthur Caesar, *Manhattan Melodrama*

Adapted Screenplay: Robert Riskin, *It Happened One Night*

Cinematography: Victor Milner, *Cleopatra*

Editing: Conrad Nervig, *Eskimo*

Original Score: Victor Schertzinger and Gus Kahn, *One Night of Love*

Original Song: "The Continental," *The Gay Divorcee*, Con Conrad, music, Herb Magidson, lyrics

Art Direction: Cedric Gibbons and Frederic Hope, *The Merry Widow*

Sound: Paul Neal, *One Night of Love*

Short subjects: (cartoon) "The Tortoise and the Hare" (Disney)
(comedy) "La Cucaracha"
(novelty) "City of Wax"

Left: Honorary Oscar® winner Shirley Temple in *The Littlest Rebel. Right:* Clark Gable and Claudette Colbert in *It Happened One Night.*

Honorary Oscar®: Shirley Temple.

Rule Changes: Editing, Song and Score awards are added. Directors are declared ineligible to win Writing Oscars®. For the first time, write–ins are allowed.

Bette Davis was President of the Academy in 1940, but she had her biggest impact on the Oscars® in 1934 by failing to receive a nomination for Best Actress for her performance in *Of Human Bondage.* Years later, in her autobiography, Davis claimed that Jack Warner had instructed Warner Brothers personnel not to nominate her.

Hollywood reaction was so persistently disbelieving that president Howard Estabrook announced that the Academy would accept write–in votes. The following year, to ensure the integrity of the nominations and the voting, control of the entire process would fall to the accounting firm of Price–Waterhouse, who count the votes to this day.

This did nothing to stop the first great Oscar® sweep, however, as Frank Capra recovered from his embarrassment of the previous year and *It Happened One Night* became the first picture to win Picture, Director, Screenplay and both acting awards. No film would duplicate that feat until *One Flew Over the Cuckoo's Nest,* forty years later. In perhaps the last recorded instance of modesty on the part of a studio executive, Columbia chief Harry Cohn, accepting the Best Picture statuette, described himself as "an innocent bystander."

1935

Picture	*Alice Adams*
	Broadway Melody of 1936
	Captain Blood
	David Copperfield
	The Informer
	Les Misérables
	Lives of a Bengal Lancer
	A Midsummer Night's Dream
	* *Mutiny on the Bounty*
	Naughty Marietta
	Ruggles of Red Gap
	Top Hat
Director	*John Ford, *The Informer*
	Henry Hathaway, *Lives of a Bengal Lancer*
	Frank Lloyd, *Mutiny on the Bounty*
Actor	Clark Gable, *Mutiny on the Bounty*
	Charles Laughton, *Mutiny on the Bounty*
	* Victor McLaglen, *The Informer*
	Franchot Tone, *Mutiny on the Bounty*
Actress	Elizabeth Bergner, *Escape Me Never*
	Claudette Colbert, *Private Worlds*
	* Bette Davis, *Dangerous*
	Katharine Hepburn, *Alice Adams*
	Miriam Hopkins, *Becky Sharp*
	Merle Oberon, *The Dark Angel*

Original Screenplay: Ben Hecht and Charles MacArthur, *The Scoundrel*

Adapted Screenplay: Dudley Nichols, *The Informer*

Cinematography: Hal Mohr, *A Midsummer Night's Dream* (write in!)

Editing: Ralph Dawson, *A Midsummer Night's Dream*

Original Score: Max Steiner, *The Informer*

Original Song: "Lullaby of Broadway," *Gold Diggers of 1935*, Harry Warren, music, Al Dubin, lyrics

Art Direction: Richard Day, *The Dark Angel*

Sound: Douglas Shearer, *Naughty Marietta*

Left: Bette Davis, Best Actress for *Dangerous. Right:* Victor McLaglen, Best Actor for *The Informer.*

Dance Direction: David Gould, *Folies Bergère*

Short subjects: (cartoon) "Three Orphan Kittens" (Disney)
    (comedy) "How To Sleep"
    (novelty) "Wings Over Everest"

Honorary Oscar®: D.W. Griffith.

Rule Changes: Dance Direction added as a category.

A tradition was born when MGM launched the first studio campaign for the Awards, taking ads for *Ah, Wilderness.* It received no nominations.

The directors left the Academy in January of 1936, two months before the awards, accusing it of failing in "every single function it has assumed. The sooner it is destroyed and forgotten, the better." Since the new Academy president was a director, this was a source of acute embarrassment to Frank Capra, who ended up getting the Academy Board of Directors to personally pick up the tab for the awards dinner.

Write–in votes were again allowed, which led Jack Warner to circulate a memo to Academy members at Warner Brothers asking them to ignore the nominations when necessary and vote a solid Warner Brothers ticket. It worked. Hal Mohr, the cinematographer of *A Midsummer Night's Dream,* became the only write–in winner in Oscar® history. Dudley Nichols refused his

Oscar®, which Capra sent him twice. For her part, Bette Davis took her Oscar® and walked out on Warner Brothers, demanding better scripts before she returned to work.

Huh? David Gould wins the Dance Direction Oscar® for *Folies Bergère* over Busby Berkeley's "Lullaby of Broadway" number from *Gold Diggers of 1935*, perhaps the greatest large scale dance number in Hollywood history.

1936

Picture	*Anthony Adverse*
	Dodsworth
	* *The Great Ziegfeld*
	Libeled Lady
	Mr. Deeds Goes to Town
	Romeo and Juliet
	San Francisco
	The Story of Louis Pasteur
	A Tale of Two Cities
	Three Smart Girls
Director	*Frank Capra, *Mr. Deeds Goes To Town*
	Gregory La Cava, *My Man Godfrey*
	Robert Z. Leonard, *The Great Ziegfeld*
	W.S. Van Dyke, *San Francisco*
	William Wyler, *Dodsworth*
Actor	Gary Cooper, *Mr. Deeds Goes To Town*
	Walter Huston, *Dodsworth*
	*Paul Muni, *The Story of Louis Pasteur*
	William Powell, *My Man Godfrey*
	Spencer Tracy, *San Francisco*
Actress	Irene Dunne, *Theodora Goes Wild*
	Gladys George, *Valiant is the Word For Carrie*
	Carole Lombard, *My Man Godfrey*
	*Luise Rainer, *The Great Ziegfeld*
	Norma Shearer, *Romeo and Juliet*
Supporting Actor	Mischa Auer, *My Man Godfrey*
	*Walter Brennan, *Come and Get It*
	Stuart Erwin, *Pigskin Parade*
	Basil Rathbone, *Romeo and Juliet*
	Akim Tamiroff, *The General Died At Dawn*
Supporting Actress	Beulah Bondi, *The Gorgeous Hussy*
	Alice Brady, *My Man Godfrey*
	Bonita Granville, *These Three*
	Maria Ouspenskaya, *Dodsworth*
	*Gale Sondergaard, *Anthony Adverse*

Original Screenplay: Robert Hopkins, *The Story of Louis Pasteur*

Left: Best Picture, *The Great Ziegfeld. Right:* Paul Muni, Best Actor for *The Story of Louis Pasteur.*

Adapted Screenplay: Pierre Gollings and Sheridan Gibney,
   The Story of Louis Pasteur

Cinematography: Gaetano Gaudio, *Anthony Adverse*

Editing: Ralph Dawson, *Anthony Adverse*

Original Score: Erich Wolfgang Korngold, *Anthony Adverse*

Original Song: "The Way You Look Tonight,"
   Swingtime—Jerome Kern, Music, Dorothy Fields, lyrics

Art Direction: Richard Day, *Dodsworth*

Sound: Douglas Shearer, *San Francisco*

Dance Direction: Seymour Felix, "A Pretty Girl is Like a
   Melody," *The Great Ziegfeld*

Short subjects: (cartoon) "Country Cousin" (Disney)
   (one–reel) "Bored of Education" (Our Gang)
   (two–reel) "The Public Pays"
   (color) "Give Me Liberty"

Honorary Oscar®: *The March of Time.*
   W. Howard Greene and Harold Rosson for the color
   cinematography of *The Garden of Allah.*

Rule Changes: Supporting Actor and Actress categories added.
Comedy shorts ditched for awards based on length—one-reel and

two-reel, and color shorts added. All English language films become eligible for picture, acting, directing and writing Oscars®.

In a move that anticipates the modern habit of having the nominating press conference at 5:30 A.M. to accommodate East Coast television, the Academy gave the press the results of the voting at eight P.M., though the awards were not given out until eleven P.M., after the dinner. MGM publicists, having heard the advance word, called Luise Rainer, nominated for *The Great Ziegfeld*, at home and ordered her to the Biltmore Hotel as soon as possible, for they had heard that she would win.

For the first time, supporting actors and actresses were honored, but did not receive statuettes, but plaques. Frank Capra continued the "Frank" domination of the director award seven of the first ten Oscar® Winners for direction were named Frank—Lloyd twice, Borzage twice, and Capra three times.

Gale Sondergaard's victory as best supporting actress in *Anthony Adverse* marked the first time anyone won an Oscar® for his or her first film. It is a surprisingly select group—after Sondergaard, it would be a decade before it happened again with Harold Russell, supporting actor, *The Best Years of Our Lives*.

The other winners for their first films include:

1949—Mercedes McCambridge, supporting actress, *All the King's Men*
1952—Shirley Booth, actress, *Come Back, Little Sheba*
1955—Paddy Chayefsky, screenplay, *Marty*
　　　Delbert Mann, director, *Marty*
　　　Jo Van Fleet, supporting actress, *East of Eden*
1957—Miyoshi Umeki, supporting actress, *Sayonara*
1968—Barbra Streisand, actress, *Funny Girl*
1973—Tatum O'Neal, *Paper Moon* (youngest Oscar® winner)
　　　John Houseman, supporting actor, *The Paper Chase*
1980—Robert Redford, director, *Ordinary People*
　　　Timothy Hutton, supporting actor, *Ordinary People*
1983—James L. Brooks, director, *Terms of Endearment*
　　　Dr. Haing S. Ngor, supporting actor, *The Killing Fields*
1986—Marlee Matlin, actress, *Children of a Lesser God*
1990—Kevin Costner, director, *Dances With Wolves*
1994—Anna Paquin, supporting actress, *The Piano*

No one has ever won best actor for their film debut, and an awful lot of these people—Russell, Umeki, Ngor, O'Neal, Houseman, Matlin—are, for one reason or another, oddities. Russell was a war vet amputee playing a war vet amputee, Ngor was a Cambodian political prisoner playing a Cambodian political prisoner, Marlee Matlin was a deaf person playing a deaf person (she is also, of course, a highly accomplished actress, but how many people in Hollywood knew that?). Of the others, Booth and Streisand were both recreating roles they played on stage.

1937

Picture	*The Awful Truth*
	Captains Courageous
	Dead End
	The Good Earth
	In Old Chicago
	* *The Life of Emile Zola*
	Lost Horizon
	100 Men And a Girl
	Stage Door
	A Star Is Born
Director	William Dieterle, *The Life of Emile Zola*
	Sidney Franklin, *The Good Earth*
	Gregory La Cava, *Stage Door*
	* Leo McCarey, *The Awful Truth*
	William Wellman, *A Star Is Born*
Actor	Charles Boyer, *Conquest*
	Fredric March, *A Star Is Born*
	Robert Montgomery, *Night Must Fall*
	Paul Muni, *The Life of Emile Zola*
	* Spencer Tracy, *Captains Courageous*
Actress	Irene Dunne, *The Awful Truth*
	Greta Garbo, *Camille*
	Janet Gaynor, *A Star Is Born*
	* Luise Rainer, *The Good Earth*
	Barbara Stanwyck, *Stella Dallas*
Supporting Actor	Ralph Bellamy, *The Awful Truth*
	Thomas Mitchell, *The Hurricane*
	* Joseph Schildkraut, *The Life of Emile Zola*
	H.B. Warner, *Lost Horizon*
	Roland Young, *Topper*
Supporting Actress	* Alice Brady, *In Old Chicago*
	Andrea Leeds, *Stage Door*
	Anne Shirley, *Stella Dallas*
	Claire Trevor, *Dead End*
	Dame May Whitty, *Night Must Fall*

Original Story: William Wellman and Robert Carson, *A Star Is Born*

Left: Spencer Tracy, Best Actor for *Captains Courageous*. *Right:* Louise Rainer, Best Actress in *The Good Earth*.

Screenplay: Heinz Herald, Geza Herczeg and Norman Reilly Raine, *The Life of Emile Zola*

Cinematography: Karl Freund, *The Good Earth*

Art Direction: Stephen Goosson, *Lost Horizon*

Editing: Gene Havlick and Gene Milford, *Lost Horizon*

Original Score: *100 Men and a Girl* (no composer credited)

Original Song: "Sweet Leilani," *Waikiki Wedding*, Harry Owen, Music and lyrics

Dance Direction: Hermes Pan, "Fun House," *Damsel in Distress*

Sound: Thomas Moulton, *The Hurricane*

Short subjects: (cartoon) "The Old Mill" (Disney)
(one–reel) "Private Life of the Gannetts"
(two–reel) "Torture Money"
(color) "Penny Wisdom" (Pete Smith specialties)

Thalberg Award: Darryl F. Zanuck

Honorary Oscar®: Mack Sennett, for his contribution to comedy screen.
Edgar Bergen, for creating Charlie McCarthy.
The Museum of Modern Art for its work in collecting films and making them available for the study of the historical and aesthetic development of the motion picture as an art form.

W. Howard Greene for the color photography of *A Star Is Born*.

Rule Changes: All members of the Actors, Directors and Writers Guilds nominate and vote. Extras vote on final ballot. Only Academy members nominate and voted for Art Direction, Cinematography, Sound and Editing. Score award voting limited to a small group of "directors, production executives, studio composers, conductors and a representative number of orchestral musicians."

Directors eligible for Writing Awards.

Irving G. Thalberg Memorial Award created.

Once a colossus bestriding Hollywood, immortalized by F. Scott Fitzgerald, who used him as the model for Monroe Stahr, the hero of *The Last Tycoon*, Irving Thalberg's legacy is the Oscar® that most often inspires people to head to the fridge. So exactly who was Irving Thalberg, and why did the Academy name an award after him?

Quite simply, Irving Thalberg formalized the conventions of the studio system as we know it. Known as the "Boy Wonder," Thalberg was Louis B. Mayer's right hand at MGM. When he died at age 36, he was widely admired as a production genius and famed as the husband of Norma Shearer, whose 1930 Oscar® victory inspired Joan Crawford's remark "What do you expect? She sleeps with the boss."

History has not been kind to Thalberg, and he is best remembered as a purveyor of well upholstered and tasteful period dramas, often directed by Sidney Franklin, for the drivel which only a star of Garbo's magnitude could transcend, and as the man who declawed the Marx Brothers and cut Erich Von Stroheim's lost masterpiece, *Greed*, from eight hours to two and had the remaining footage rendered for its silver content. Given the fact that it is the Award bearing Thalberg's name that goes to producers of long and honorable service, a half-sinister meaning accrues to the Oscar® statuette—a man plunging a sword into a reel of film.

His final productions, *Camille* and *The Good Earth*, were ghosts at the banquet at the 1937 Oscars®, the former for Garbo's greatest performance, the latter winning best actress and cinematography. Otherwise, '38 was a year for seeing double—Luise Rainer won her second consecutive (and last) Oscar®. Rainer never worked in pictures again, reeling from an attack of second rate scripts and the breakup of her marriage to playwright Clifford Odets. Leo McCarey, honored for his direction of one of the greatest screwball comedies, muttered that "You gave it to me for the wrong picture," himself preferring *Make Way For Tomorrow*, a serious drama about old age.

Odd fates of Oscar® winners, 2: Cinematographer Karl Freund, one of the giants of the German silent cinema (F.W. Murnau's *The Last Laugh*, Fritz Lang's *Metropolis*, etc.) spent the final years of his career as director of photography on *I Love Lucy*.

1938

Picture	The Adventures of Robin Hood
	Alexander's Ragtime Band
	Boys Town
	The Citadel
	Four Daughters
	Grand Illusion
	Jezebel
	Pygmalion
	Test Pilot
	* You Can't Take It With You
Director	* Frank Capra, You Can't Take It With You
	Michael Curtiz, Angels With Dirty Faces
	Michael Curtiz, Four Daughters
	Norman Taurog, Boys Town
	King Vidor, The Citadel
Actor	Charles Boyer, Algiers
	James Cagney, Angels With Dirty Faces
	Robert Donat, The Citadel
	Leslie Howard, Pygmalion
	* Spencer Tracy, Boys Town
Actress	Fay Bainter, White Banners
	* Bette Davis, Jezebel
	Wendy Hiller, Pygmalion
	Norma Shearer, Marie Antoinette
	Margaret Sullavan, Three Comrades
Supporting Actor	* Walter Brennan, Kentucky
	John Garfield, Four Daughters
	Gene Lockhart, Algiers
	Robert Morley, Marie Antoinette
	Basil Rathbone, If I Were King
Supporting Actress	* Fay Bainter, Jezebel
	Beulah Bondi, Of Human Hearts
	Billie Burke, Merrily We Live
	Spring Byington, You Can't Take It With You
	Miliza Korjus, The Great Waltz

Left: Bette Davis, Best Actress for *Jezebel*, with co-star Henry Fonda. *Right:* Walter Brennan, Best Supporting Actor in *Kentucky*.

Original Story: Eleonore Griffin and Dore Schary, *Boys Town*

Screenplay: George Bernard Shaw, adaptation by Ian Dalrymple, Cecil Lewis and W.P. Lipscombe, *Pygmalion*

Cinematography: Joseph Ruttenberg, *The Great Waltz*

Editing: Ralph Dawson, *The Adventures of Robin Hood*

Original Score: Alfred Newman, *Alexander's Ragtime Band*

Original Song: "Thanks for the Memory," *Big Broadcast of 1938.* Ralph Bainger, music, Leo Robin, lyrics

Art Direction: Carl J. Weyl, *The Adventures of Robin Hood*

Sound: Thomas Moulton, *The Cowboy and the Lady*

Short subjects: (cartoon) "Ferdinand the Bull" (Disney) (one–reel) "That Mothers Might Live" (two–reel) "Declaration of Independence"

Thalberg Award: Hal Wallis

Honorary Oscar®: Deanna Durbin and Mickey Rooney for bringing the spirit and personification of youth to the screen.
Harry B. Warner for producing historical Short subjects.
Walt Disney for *Snow White and the Seven Dwarfs.*
Oliver Marsh and Allen Davey for the color cinematography of *Sweethearts.*

The special effects crew on *Spawn of the North*.
J. Arthur Ball for contributions to color cinematography.

Rule Changes: Score award divided into Score and Original Score. Extras are not allowed to vote for Best Song. Assistant Director and Dance Direction prizes discontinued.

One wonders if people at the 1938 awards thought they were having a flashback—Spencer Tracy won his second Best Actor Oscar®, Bette Davis her second Best Actress, and Walter Brennan his second Supporting Actor Oscar® (and the category was only three years old!). For that matter, Frank Capra won his third directing Oscar®.

Capra was the story in 1938. The Directors' Guild, with whom Capra had gone to war over their boycott of the Oscars®, decided that Capra had done such a good job with the Academy that they elected him president of the Guild. When Nicholas Schenck, head of the producers' association wouldn't recognize the Guild as the sole negotiating agent for the directors, Capra resigned as president of the Academy, called for a strike, and threatened a boycott of the Academy Awards®. The producers folded.

Jean Renoir's *Grand Illusion*, a film which touched the pacifist/isolationist mood of the times and came complete with an unexpected endorsement from President Roosevelt, became the first foreign language film nominated for best picture.

Picture	*Dark Victory*
	*Gone With the Wind
	Goodbye Mr. Chips
	Love Affair
	Mr. Smith Goes To Washington
	Ninotchka
	Of Mice and Men
	Stagecoach
	The Wizard of Oz
	Wuthering Heights

Director	Frank Capra, *Mr. Smith Goes To Washington*
	*Victor Fleming, *Gone With the Wind*
	John Ford, *Stagecoach*
	Sam Wood, *Goodbye, Mr. Chips*
	William Wyler, *Wuthering Heights*

Actor	*Robert Donat, *Goodbye Mr. Chips*
	Clark Gable, *Gone With the Wind*
	Laurence Olivier, *Wuthering Heights*
	Mickey Rooney, *Babes in Arms*
	James Stewart, *Mr. Smith Goes To Washington*

Actress	Bette Davis, *Dark Victory*
	Irene Dunne, *Love Affair*
	Greta Garbo, *Ninotchka*
	Greer Garson, *Goodbye Mr. Chips*
	*Vivien Leigh, *Gone With the Wind*

Supporting Actor	Brian Aherne, *Juarez*
	Harry Carey, *Mr. Smith Goes To Washington*
	Brian Donlevy, *Beau Geste*
	*Thomas Mitchell, *Stagecoach*
	Claude Rains, *Mr. Smith Goes To Washington*

Supporting Actress	Olivia de Havilland, *Gone With the Wind*
	Geraldine Fitzgerald, *Wuthering Heights*
	*Hattie McDaniel, *Gone With the Wind*
	Edna May Oliver, *Drums Along the Mohawk*
	Maria Ouspenskaya, *Love Affair*

Original Story: Lewis R. Foster, *Mr. Smith Goes To Washington*

Screenplay: Sidney Howard, *Gone With the Wind*

Cinematography: (black and white) Gregg Toland, *Wuthering Heights*

Left: Clark Gable and Vivien Leigh in the Best Picture winner, *Gone With the Wind. Right:* *The Wizard of Oz,* which featured the Best Song, "Over the Rainbow."

(color) Ernest Haller and Ray Rennahan, *Gone With the Wind*

Editing: Hal C. Kern and James E. Newcom, *Gone With the Wind*

Score: Richard Hageman, Frank Harling, John Leipold and Leo Shuken, *Stagecoach*

Original Score: Herbert Strothart, *The Wizard of Oz*

Original Song: "Over The Rainbow," *The Wizard of Oz,* Harold Arlen, music, E.Y. Harburg, lyrics

Art Direction: Lyle Wheeler, *Gone With the Wind*

Sound: Bernard B. Brown, *When Tomorrow Comes*

Special Effects: E.H. Hanson (visual), Edwin C. Hahn (sound), *The Rains Came*

Short subjects: (cartoon) "The Ugly Duckling" (Disney) (one–reel) "Busy Little Bears" (two–reels) "Sons of Liberty"

Thalberg Award: David O. Selznick

Honorary Oscar®: Douglas Fairbanks, first President of the Academy.
The Motion Picture Relief Fund, for outstanding service to the industry.

Judy Garland, outstanding juvenile performance.

William Cameron Menzies for use of color in *Gone With the Wind*.

The Technicolor Company.

Rule Changes: Special effects added as an award category. Cinematography now a double award, for black and white and color cinematography. English language films are eligible in all categories. Directors can only be nominated for one film in a year.

Today, we take Oscar® Sweeps for granted—for a *Gandhi* or a *Last Emperor* to win eight or nine Oscars® strikes us as nothing unusual. For the Oscar® voters of 1939, the overwhelming performance, production costs and eventual Awards sweep of *Gone With the Wind* was something completely new, if not altogether unexpected. Producer David O. Selznick had kept Hollywood on the boil for almost three years with his epic production of Margaret Mitchell's best-selling novel.

Gone With the Wind did not merely win more Oscars® than any previous film—eight competitively, plus the Thalberg Award for Selznick, and a special Oscar® for William Cameron Menzies colorful art direction—but unleashed a series of other firsts. Hattie McDaniel became the first black actress to win an Oscar® (and the first African–American nominee in any category, and the first African–American to attend the Oscars® as a guest). Credited screenwriter Sidney Howard (there were a dozen writers, including Ben Hecht) became the first posthumous Oscar®-winner. Shortly before the awards, he was run over by a tractor on his Massachusetts farm—making him the first, and perhaps only Oscar®-winner to suffer death by agricultural implement.

There were two other firsts in 1939. Bob Hope debuted as master of ceremonies and the *Los Angeles Times* broke its word to the Academy and published the winners in their early evening edition—two hours before the Awards were handed out. From that point on, nobody would know who won, except for the men from Price–Waterhouse.

Picture	*All This, And Heaven Too* *Foreign Correspondent* *The Grapes of Wrath* *The Great Dictator* *Kitty Foyle* *The Letter* *The Long Voyage Home* *Our Town* *The Philadelphia Story* * *Rebecca*
Director	George Cukor, *The Philadelphia Story* * John Ford, *The Grapes of Wrath* Alfred Hitchcock, *Rebecca* Sam Wood, *Kitty Foyle* William Wyler, *The Letter*
Actor	Charles Chaplin, *The Great Dictator* Henry Fonda, *The Grapes of Wrath* Raymond Massey, *Abe Lincoln in Illinois* Laurence Olivier, *Rebecca* * James Stewart, *The Philadelphia Story*
Actress	Bette Davis, *The Letter* Joan Fontaine, *Rebecca* Katharine Hepburn, *The Philadelphia Story* * Ginger Rogers, *Kitty Foyle* Martha Scott, *Our Town*
Supporting Actor	Albert Basserman, *Foreign Correspondent* * Walter Brennan, *The Westerner* William Gargan, *They Knew What They Wanted* Jack Oakie, *The Great Dictator* James Stephenson, *The Letter*
Supporting Actress	Judith Anderson, *Rebecca* * Jane Darwell, *The Grapes of Wrath* Ruth Hussey, *The Philadelphia Story* Barbara O'Neil, *All This and Heaven Too* Marjorie Rambeau, *Primrose Path*

Left: Ginger Rogers, Best Actress for *Kitty Foyle. Right:* James Stewart, Best Actor in *The Philadelphia Story,* with Katharine Hepburn.

Original Story: Benjamin Glazer and John S. Toldy, *Arise, My Love*

Original Screenplay: Preston Sturges, *The Great McGinty*

Screenplay: Donald Ogden Stewart, *The Thief of Bagdad*

Cinematography: (black and white) George Barnes, *Rebecca* (color) George Perinal, *The Thief of Bagdad*

Editing: Anne Bauchens, *Northwest Mounted Police*

Score: Alfred Newman, *Tin Pan Alley*

Original Score: Leigh Harline, Paul Smith and Ned Washington, *Pinocchio*

Original Song: "When You Wish Upon A Star," *Pinocchio,* Leigh Harline, music, Ned Washington, lyrics

Interior Decoration: (black and white) Cedric Gibbons and Paul Groesse, *Pride and Prejudice* (color) Vincent Korda, *The Thief of Bagdad*

Sound: Douglas Shearer, *Strike Up The Band*

Short subjects: (cartoon) "Milky Way" (one–reel) "Quicker 'n a Wink" (two–reel) "Teddy, the Rough Rider"

Special Effects: *The Thief of Bagdad,* Lawrence Butler (visual), Jack Whitney (sound)

Thalberg Award: Not given

Honorary Oscar®: Bob Hope, in recognition of his services to
the industry.
  Colonel Nathan Levinson for his service to the industry.

When Bob Hope came out to MC the show, he looked at all the
Oscars® on the dais (in those days, all the Oscars® sat on a table
on the stage) and joked, "Did Selznick send them back?" refer-
ring, of course, to Selznick's great sweep the year before with *Gone
With the Wind*. He hadn't, of course, but had he returned them,
he would have been hoping to take them all home, as Selznick's
production of *Rebecca* had eleven nominations. Despite Selznick's
best efforts—in those pre-video days, he actually held a second
premiere for *Rebecca*, which had closed months before, to draw
community attention to it—*Rebecca*'s eleven nominations yielded
only one Oscar®, for best picture.
  For the first time, the President of the United States addressed
the awards supper via radio hook–up, praising the film industry
for its promotion of the American way of life.
  The evening's humor was provided mostly by the winners of the
writing Oscars®—Preston Sturges (*The Great McGinty*) accepted
his award noting that he was accepting the award on behalf of
Preston Sturges. Donald Ogden Stewart noted that he and he
alone was responsible for the success of *The Philadelphia Story*.
  Jimmy Stewart was the only acting nominee to show up at the
dinner, so it's a good thing he won (for the third best performance
in *The Philadelphia Story*—Hepburn didn't win and Cary Grant
wasn't even nominated), as much, people say, for his overlooked
performance in 1939's *Mr. Smith Goes To Washington* as for *The
Philadelphia Story*. On orders of his father, he sent his Oscar®
back to the family hardware store in Pennsylvania.

Picture	*Blossoms in the Dust*
	Citizen Kane
	Here Comes Mr. Jordan
	Hold Back the Dawn
	* How Green Was My Valley
	The Little Foxes
	The Maltese Falcon
	One Foot in Heaven
	Sergeant York
	Suspicion
Director	*John Ford, *How Green Was My Valley*
	Alexander Hall, *Here Comes Mr. Jordan*
	Howard Hawks, *Sergeant York*
	Orson Welles, *Citizen Kane*
	William Wyler, *The Little Foxes*
Actor	*Gary Cooper, *Sergeant York*
	Cary Grant, *Penny Serenade*
	Walter Huston, *The Devil and Daniel Webster*
	Robert Montgomery, *Here Comes Mr. Jordan*
	Orson Welles, *Citizen Kane*
Actress	Bette Davis, *The Little Foxes*
	*Joan Fontaine, *Suspicion*
	Greer Garson, *Blossoms in the Dust*
	Olivia de Havilland, *Hold Back the Dawn*
	Barbara Stanwyck, *Ball of Fire*
Supporting Actor	Walter Brennan, *Sergeant York*
	Charles Coburn, *The Devil and Miss Jones*
	*Donald Crisp, *How Green Was My Valley*
	James Gleason, *Here Comes Mr. Jordan*
	Sydney Greenstreet, *The Maltese Falcon*
Supporting Actress	Sara Allgood, *How Green Was My Valley*

*Mary Astor, *The Great Lie*
Patricia Collinge, *The Little Foxes*
Teresa Wright, *The Little Foxes*
Margaret Wycherly, *Sergeant York*

Original Story: Harry Segall, *Here Comes Mr. Jordan*

Original Screenplay: Herman J. Mankiewicz and Orson Welles, *Citizen Kane*

Screenplay: Sidney Buchman and Seton I. Miller, *Here Comes Mr. Jordan*

Cinematography: (black and white) Arthur Miller, *How Green Was My Valley*
(color) Ernest Palmer and Ray Rennahan, *Blood and Sand*

Editing: William Holmes, *Sergeant York*

Score: (dramatic picture) Bernard Herrmann, *All That Money Can Buy*

Score: (musical) Frank Churchill and Oliver Wallace, *Dumbo*

Original Song: "The Last Time I Saw Paris," *Lady Be Good*, Jerome Kern, music, Oscar Hammerstein II, lyrics

Art Direction: (black and white) *How Green Was My Valley*
(color) Cedric Gibbons, Urie McCleary, *Blossoms in the Dust*

Sound: Jack Whitney, *That Hamilton Woman*

Special Effects: Farciot Edouard and Gordon Jennings (visual), Louis Mesenkop (sound), *I Wanted Wings*

Short subjects: (cartoon) "Lend A Paw" (Disney)
(one–reel) "Of Pups and Puzzles"
(two–reel) "Main Street on the March"

Documentary: "Churchill's Island"

Thalberg Award: Walt Disney

Honorary Oscar®: Ray Scott, for the documentary *Kukan*, filmed in China at war.
The British Ministry of Information for its documentary film *Target For Tonight*.
Leopold Stokowski and Walt Disney for *Fantasia*.

Rule Changes: The category of Documentary added. The Score and Original Score categories were revised to Scoring of a Dramatic Picture and Scoring of a Musical Picture.

Left: Orson Welles and Joseph Cotton in *Citizen Kane*, winner of the Best Screenplay Oscar®. *Right:* Gary Cooper, Best Actor winner for *Sergeant York*.

Hollywood goes to war. Or, at least, Hollywood is confused by the war. New Academy President Bette Davis suggests that the Awards be held in a theater, with tickets sold to the public, that the proceeds go to British war relief, and that the stars should not wear glamorous evening gowns. The Academy didn't like any of these changes, so Davis resigned. They did have a banquet, however, despite some fears that the Japanese might launch an air raid on Los Angeles.

The big nominees were *Seargeant York* (11), *How Green Was My Valley* (10) and *Citizen Kane* (9). The legendary injustice of the '41 Oscars® was the defeat of *Citizen Kane* by the forces of evil (Louella Parsons) and *How Green Was My Valley*. This ignores two things which militated against the Welles' classic. First, it didn't make any money. Second, *Kane* is a dark film, where *How Green Was My Valley* is heartwarming in the best Hollywood manner. Finally, Welles spent a good deal of time running Hollywood down—producers were "overpaid office boys," for example. Hollywood seldom feeds the hand that bites it.

The best story, however, was the battle of the sisters, Joan Fontaine and Olivia de Havilland, whose life-long feud really crystallized when Fontaine's performance in *Suspicion* was chosen over de Havilland's in *Hold Back the Dawn*. (Forty years later, at the Montreal Film Festival, Fontaine would say that there was no feud, but it was de Havilland's fault.)

Huh? Bernard Herrmann wrote some of the greatest film scores of all time, ranging from *Citizen Kane* and *The Magnifi-*

cent Ambersons to *Vertigo, Rear Window, Psycho* and *North by Northwest* for Hitchcock to, at the very end of his career, *Taxi Driver*. He won his single Oscar® in 1941 for *All That Money Can Buy*.

Picture: *The Invaders*
Kings Row
The Magnificent Ambersons
* *Mrs. Miniver*
The Pied Piper
The Pride of the Yankees
Random Harvest
The Talk of the Town
Wake Island
Yankee Doodle Dandy

Director: Michael Curtiz, *Yankee Doodle Dandy*
John Farrow, *Wake Island*
Mervyn LeRoy, *Random Harvest*
Sam Wood, *Kings Row*
* William Wyler, *Mrs. Miniver*

Actor: *James Cagney, *Yankee Doodle Dandy*
Ronald Colman, *Random Harvest*
Gary Cooper in *The Pride of the
Yankees*
Walter Pidgeon, *Mrs. Miniver*
Monty Woolley, *The Pied Piper*

Actress: Bette Davis, *Now Voyager*
* Greer Garson, *Mrs. Miniver*
Katherine Hepburn, *Woman of the
Year*
Rosalind Russell, *My Sister Eileen*
Teresa Wright, *The Pride of the
Yankees*

Supporting Actor: William Bendix, *Wake Island*
* Van Heflin, *Johnny Eager*
Walter Huston, *Yankee Doodle Dandy*
Frank Morgan, *Tortilla Flat*
Henry Travers, *Mrs. Miniver*

Supporting Actress: Gladys Cooper, *Now, Voyager*
Agnes Moorehead, *The Magnificent
Ambersons*
Susan Peters, *Random Harvest*
Dame May Whitty, *Mrs. Miniver*
* Teresa Wright, *Mrs. Miniver*

Left: Jimmy Cagney, Best Actor, *Yankee Doodle Dandy. Right:* Greer Garson, Best Actress for *Mrs. Miniver.*

Original Story: Emeric Pressburger, *The Invaders*

Original Screenplay: Michael Kanin and Ring Lardner, Jr., *Woman of the Year*

Screenplay: George Froeschel, James Hilton, Claudine West and Arthur Wimperis, *Mrs. Miniver*

Cinematography: (black and white) Joseph Ruttenberg, *Mrs. Miniver*
(color) Leon Shamroy, *The Black Swan*

Editing: Daniel Mandell, *The Pride of the Yankees*

Score: (drama) Max Steiner, *Now Voyager*
(musical) Ray Heindorf, Heinz Roemheld, *Yankee Doodle Dandy*

Original Song: "White Christmas," *Holiday Inn,* Irving Berlin

Art Direction: (black and white) Richard Day, Joseph Wright, *This Above All*
(color) Richard Day, Joseph Wright, *My Gal Sal*

Sound: Nathan Levinson, *Yankee Doodle Dandy*

Documentary: "The Battle of Midway" (John Ford)
"Kokoda Front Line"
"Moscow Strikes Back"
"Prelude to War"

Yes, an unprecedented and never equalled four winners.

Special Effects: Farciout Edouart, Gordon Jennings and
William L. Pereira (visual), Louis Mesenkop (sound),
Reap the Wild Wind

Short subjects: (cartoon) "Der Fuehrer's Face" (Disney)
(one–reel) "Speaking of Animals and Their Families"
(two–reel) "Beyond the Line of Duty"

Thalberg Award: Sidney Franklin

Honorary Oscar®: Charles Boyer, for establishing the French
Research Foundation in Los Angeles.
Noel Coward, for *In Which We Serve*.
MGM for the Andy Hardy series.

One of Hollywood's great contributions to the war effort came
when they decided to help fight wartime metal shortages and
make the statuettes of plaster. The other, rather bizarre contribution to the war effort came in the geometrically expanded nomination list for the Best Documentary category—25 nominations, all
for war–themed documentaries, with four winners.

The legend which arose from the Awards ceremony was that
Greer Garson's acceptance speech ran for over an hour. She actually spoke for about seven minutes, not bad for someone who's
opening line was "I'm practically unprepared," and her speech
remains the longest to this day. Richard Attenborough's *Ghandi*
speech only seemed longer.

The most startling nominations were the quartet for *The Magnificent Ambersons*, Orson Welles' follow–up to *Citizen Kane*.
While Welles was in South America scouting locations and shooting footage for *It's All True*, a project which never came to frui-
tion, RKO decided to put Welles in his place. After unfavorable
previews, the studio cut the film from 128 minutes to 88 minutes
(rendering the leftover footage for its silver content) and opened
it on the bottom of a double–bill with *Mexican Spitfire Sees A
Ghost*. In its degraded state *The Magnificent Ambersons* remains
the best film of its year, and some people in Hollywood did take
note. Agnes Moorehead, particularly, gave the performance of a
lifetime.

Picture	*Casablanca
	For Whom The Bell Tolls
	Heaven Can Wait
	The Human Comedy
	In Which We Serve
	Madame Curie
	The More the Merrier
	The Ox-Bow Incident
	The Song of Bernadette
	Watch on the Rhine

Director Clarence Brown, *The Human Comedy*
         *Michael Curtiz, *Casablanca*
          Henry King, *The Song of Bernadette*
          Ernst Lubitsch, *Heaven Can Wait*
          George Stevens, *The More the Merrier*

Actor   Humphrey Bogart, *Casablanca*
          Gary Cooper, *For Whom The Bell Tolls*
         *Paul Lukas, *Watch on the Rhine*
          Walter Pidgeon, *Madame Curie*
          Mickey Rooney, *The Human Comedy*

Actress Jean Arthur, *The More the Merrier*
          Ingrid Bergman, *For Whom The Bell Tolls*
          Joan Fontaine, *The Constant Nymph*
          Greer Garson, *Madame Curie*
         *Jennifer Jones, *The Song of Bernadette*

Supporting Actor Charles Bickford, *The Song of Bernadette*
                 *Charles Coburn, *The More the Merrier*
                  J. Carrol Naish, *Sahara*
                  Claude Rains, *Casablanca*
                  Akim Tamiroff, *For Whom The Bell Tolls*

Supporting Actress Gladys Cooper, *The Song of Bernadette*
                    Paulette Goddard, *So Proudly We Hail*
                   *Katina Paxinou, *For Whom The Bell Tolls*
                    Anne Revere, *The Song of Bernadette*
                    Lucille Watson, *Watch on the Rhine*

Left: Humphrey Bogart and Ingrid Bergman in Best Picture, *Casablanca. Right:* Jennifer Jones, Best Actress in *The Song of Bernadette.*

Original Story: William Saroyan, *The Human Comedy*

Original Screenplay: Norman Krasna, *The Princess O'Rourke*

Screenplay: Julius J. Epstein, Philip G. Epstein and Howard Koch, *Casablanca*

Cinematography: (black and white) Arthur Miller, *The Song of Bernadette*
(color) Hal Mohr and W. Howard Greene, *The Phantom of the Opera*

Editing: George Amy, *Air Force*

Score, dramatic or comedy picture: Alfred Newman, *The Song of Bernadette*

Score, musical picture: Ray Heindorf, *This Is the Army*

Original Song: "You'll Never Know," *Hello, Frisco, Hello,* Harry Warren, music, Mack Gordon, lyrics

Art Direction: (black and white) James Basevi, *The Song of Bernadette*
(color) Alexander Golitzen, John B. Goodman, *The Phantom of the Opera*

Sound: Stephen Dunne, *This Land is Mine*

Short subjects: (cartoon) "Yankee Doodle Mouse"
(one-reel) "Amphibious Fighters"
(two-reel) "Heavenly Music"

Documentary: (feature) *Desert Victory*
  (short) "December 7th"

Special Effects: *Crash Dive*, Fred Sersen (visual), Roger
  Heman (sound)

Thalberg Award: Hal B. Wallis

Honorary Oscar®: George Pal for the development of
  Puppetoons.

World War II was still raging, and the Academy held the awards
in a theatre—Grauman's (now Mann's) Chinese, cancelled the
dinner and handed out passes to 200 servicemen. They did not,
however, give the proceeds to charity. Instead of speeches, for the
first time the Academy Awards® show offered variety acts. On the
other hand, putting the show in a public theatre rather than a
hotel meant that the stars had to park their own cars.

The radio broadcast did not begin until the acting awards were
given, so the directors were angry and threatened, once again, to
leave the Academy. They didn't, of course.

The surprise winner was Jennifer Jones, the Selznick protégée
who starred in *Song of Bernadette*, a 160 minute film about a
young girl who sees the Virgin Mary (played in the film by Linda
Darnell!). Most prognosticators had their money on Ingrid Bergman's performance in *For Whom the Bell Tolls*, backed by her
immortal turn in *Casablanca*. Jones, celebrating her birthday on
Oscar® night, apologized to Bergman for winning.

Looking back at that performance, one sees that most of the
credit should go to Oscar®–winning cinematographer Arthur
Miller, who managed to light Jones better than any cameraman
since and makes her look exceptionally tremulous and innocent.

1944

Picture	*Double Indemnity*
	Gaslight
	* *Going My Way*
	Since You Went Away
	Wilson
Director	Alfred Hitchcock, *Lifeboat*
	Henry King, *Wilson*
	*Leo McCarey, *Going My Way*
	Otto Preminger, *Laura*
	Billy Wilder, *Double Indemnity*
Actor	Charles Boyer, *Gaslight*
	*Bing Crosby, *Going My Way*
	Barry Fitzgerald, *Going My Way*
	Cary Grant, *None But the Lonely Heart*
	Alexander Knox, *Wilson*
Actress	*Ingrid Bergman, *Gaslight*
	Claudette Colbert, *Since You Went Away*
	Bette Davis, *Mr. Skeffington*
	Greer Garson, *Mrs. Parkington*
	Barbara Stanwyck, *Double Indemnity*
Supporting Actor	Hume Cronyn, *The Seventh Cross*
	*Barry Fitzgerald, *Going My Way*
	Claude Rains, *Mr. Skeffington*
	Clifton Webb, *Laura*
	Monty Woolley, *Since You Went Away*
Supporting Actress	*Ethel Barrymore, *None But The Lonely Heart*
	Jennifer Jones, *Since You Went Away*
	Angela Lansbury, *Gaslight*
	Aline MacMahon, *Dragon Seed*
	Agnes Moorehead, *Mrs. Parkington*

Original Story: Leo McCarey, *Going My Way*

Original Screenplay: Lamar Trotti, *Wilson*

Screenplay: Frank Butler and Frank Cavatt, *Going My Way*

Cinematography: (black and white) Joseph LaShelle, *Laura*
  (color) Leon Shamroy, *Wilson*

Left: Bing Crosby, Best Actor for *Going My Way,* with Jean Heather. *Right:* Ingrid Bergman, Best Actress for *Gaslight,* with Charles Boyer.

Editing: Barbara MacLean, *Wilson*

Original Score: (dramatic or comedy picture) Max Steiner, *Since You Went Away*
(musical picture) Carmen Dragon and Morris Stoloff, *Cover Girl*

Original Song: "Swinging on a Star," *Going My Way,* James Van Heusen, music, Johnny Burke, lyrics

Art Decoration: (black and white) Cedric Gibbons and Eilliam Ferrari, *Gaslight*
(color) Wiard Ihnen, *Wilson*

Sound: E.H. Hansen, *Wilson*

Documentary: (feature) *The Fighting Lady*
(short) "With the Marines at Tarawa"

Short subjects: (cartoon) "Mouse Trouble"
(one–reel) "Who's Who in Animal Land"
(two–reel) "I Won't Play"

Special Effects: *Thirty Seconds Over Tokyo,* Arnold Gillespie, Donald Jahraus, Warren Newcombe (Photographic), Roger Heman, Sound

Thalberg Award: Darryl F. Zanuck

Honorary Oscar®: Margaret O'Brien, outstanding child actress.

Bob Hope, for his services to the Academy.

Rule Changes: The Best Picture category was limited to five nominees. Extras no longer were allowed to vote.

Going My Way and Darryl F. Zanuck's *Wilson* dominated the nominations with ten each, though the tie was achieved through one of the great oddities of Oscar® history, the first and only time an actor was nominated twice for the same performance—Barry Fitzgerald's nomination as both actor and supporting actor in *Going My Way*. It was perfectly within the rules of the Academy, but afterwards the rules were changed to prevent it. Fitzgerald won best supporting actor, as people with simultaneous nominations did until Sigourney Weaver broke the mold by losing for both *Gorillas in The Mist* and *Working Girl* and Al Pacino won for his lead performance in *Scent of a Woman* and lost his supporting performance in *Glengarry Glen Ross*.

The enormous success of *Going My Way* led to another historic first—one that, in later years, would not seem an oddity at all—Leo McCarey became the first man to win the directing and writing Oscars® in the same year. It is intriguing that McCarey, an old–line Hollywood director, would be the first to pull off this parlay, rather than the crop of writer–directors who emerged in the '40s. Of course, McCarey would soon be followed by John Huston, Billy Wilder and Joseph L. Mankiewicz.

Ingrid Bergman's Oscar® for *Gaslight,* like Jimmy Stewart's in 1940 for *The Philadelphia Story,* was viewed largely as a make–up Oscar®. Given Barbara Stanwyck's performance in *Double Indemnity,* it's a shame the Academy never felt the need to give her a competitive Oscar®.

Picture	*Anchors Aweigh*
	The Bells of St. Mary's
	* *The Lost Weekend*
	Mildred Pierce
	Spellbound
Director	Clarence Brown, *National Velvet*
	Alfred Hitchcock, *Spellbound*
	Leo McCarey, *Bells of St. Mary's*
	Jean Renoir, *The Southerner*
	* Billy Wilder, *The Lost Weekend*
Actor	Bing Crosby, *The Bells of St. Mary's*
	Gene Kelly, *Anchors Aweigh*
	* Ray Milland, *The Lost Weekend*
	Gregory Peck, *The Keys of the Kingdom*
	Cornel Wilde, *A Song to Remember*
Actress	Ingrid Bergman, *The Bells of St. Mary's*
	* Joan Crawford, *Mildred Pierce*
	Greer Garson, *Valley of Decision*
	Jennifer Jones, *Love Letters*
	Gene Tierney, *Leave Her to Heaven*
Supporting Actor	Michael Chekhov, *Spellbound*
	John Dall, *The Corn is Green*
	* James Dunn, *A Tree Grows in Brooklyn*
	Robert Mitchum, *The Story of G.I. Joe*
	J. Carrol Naish, *A Medal for Benny*
Supporting Actress	Eve Arden, *Mildred Pierce*
	Ann Blyth, *Mildred Pierce*
	Angela Lansbury, *The Picture of Dorian Gray*
	Joan Lorring, *The Corn is Green*
	* Anne Revere, *National Velvet*

Original Story: Charles G. Booth, *The House on 92nd Street*

Original Screenplay: Richard Schweizer, *Marie–Louise*

Screenplay: Charles Brackett and Billy Wilder, *The Lost Weekend*

Left: Billy Wilder, Best Director for *The Lost Weekend. Right:* Joan Crawford, Best Actress, *Mildred Pierce.*

Cinematography: (black and white) Harry Stradling, *The Picture of Dorian Grey*
(color) Leon Shamroy, *Leave Her To Heaven*

Editing: Robert J. Kern, *National Velvet*

Original Score: (dramatic or comedy picture) Miklos Rosza, *Spellbound*
(musical picture) Georgie Stoll, *Anchors Aweigh*

Original Song: "It Might as Well Be Spring," *State Fair*, Richard Rodgers, music, Oscar Hammerstein II, lyrics

Interior Decoration: (color) Hans Dreier and Ernst Fegte, *Frenchman's Creek*
(black and white) Wiard Ihnen, *Blood on the Sun*

Sound: Stephen Dunne, *Bells of St. Mary's*

Short subjects: (cartoon) "Quiet Please" (Tom & Jerry)
(one–reel) "Stairway to Light"
(two–reel) "Star in the Night"

Documentary: (feature) *The True Glory*
(short) "Hitler Lives"

Special Effects: *Wonder Man*, John Fulton (photography), A.W. Johns (sound)

Thalberg Award: Not given

Honorary Oscar®: Walter Wanger, for six years service as
    president of the Academy.
    Peggy Ann Garner, outstanding child actress.
    "The House I Live In," a short subject on tolerance.
    Republic Studio, for building an outstanding music scoring
    auditorium.

The first post–war Oscar® winners indicate the beginnings of a
small seismic shift in the Academy Awards®. *The Lost Weekend*
was the sort of film that did not usually win. Where big Oscar®
winners had once been corporate and big—the Selznick–Zanuck
school of thought, *The Lost Weekend* was a small film and, more
important, a personal film. Wilder had found the project, pitched
it to Paramount, brought his own writing partner in to co–write
and produce (Charles Brackett). It is quite possible that the win
was actually a result of the Academy membership being blinded
by the social significance of alcoholism as a subject matter. The
'40s were the decade of the socially responsible Oscar® winner:
*The Lost Weekend, Mrs. Miniver, Gentlemen's Agreement, All the
King's Men. The Lost Weekend*'s victory is a blip on the horizon,
but it does open the door for some of the smaller winners. Billy
Wilder, by the by, was presented with his Oscar® by William
Wyler.

The 1945 Oscars® are perhaps most famous, though, for the
victory of Joan Crawford as best actress in *Mildred Pierce*. For
the post–*Mommie Dearest* generation, it does contain that sub-
limely camp moment when Mildred looks at her daughter and
asks "Afraid of your own mother?" The night of the Oscars®,
Crawford claimed that she was too ill to attend. As many, including daughter Christina have noted, she was suffering from a mon-
strous case of stage fright. She made a remarkable recovery upon
winning, and was able to receive the statuette at home from
director Michael Curtiz shortly after the Awards show. This was
the same Michael Curtiz who responded to news of her casting by
saying that he didn't want to work with "a has–been."

1946

Picture	*The Best Years of Our Lives*
	Henry V
	It's a Wonderful Life
	The Razor's Edge
	The Yearling
Director	Clarence Brown, *The Yearling*
	Frank Capra, *It's a Wonderful Life*
	David Lean, *Brief Encounter*
	Robert Siodmak, *The Killers*
	*William Wyler, *The Best Years of Our Lives*
Actor	*Fredric March, *The Best Years of Our Lives*
	Laurence Olivier, *Henry V*
	Larry Parks, *The Jolson Story*
	Gregory Peck, *The Yearling*
	James Stewart, *It's a Wonderful Life*
Actress	*Olivia de Havilland, *To Each His Own*
	Celia Johnson, *Brief Encounter*
	Jennifer Jones, *Duel in the Sun*
	Rosalind Russell, *Sister Kenny*
	Jane Wyman, *The Yearling*
Supporting Actor	Charles Coburn, *The Green Years*
	William Demarest, *The Jolson Story*
	Claude Rains, *Notorious*
	*Harold Russell, *The Best Years of Our Lives*
	Clifton Webb, *The Razor's Edge*
Supporting Actress	Ethel Barrymore, *The Spiral Staircase*
	*Anne Baxter, *The Razor's Edge*
	Lillian Gish, *Duel in the Sun*
	Flora Robson, *Saratoga Trunk*
	Gale Sondergaard, *Anna and the King of Siam*

Original Story: Clemence Dane, *Vacation from Marriage*

Original Screenplay: Muriel Box and Sidney Box, *The Seventh Veil*

Screenplay: Robert E. Sherwood, *The Best Years of Our Lives*

90

Left: Best Supporting Actor Harold Russell, Dana Andrews, and Best Actor Fredric March in *The Best Years of Our Lives. Right:* Best Actress Olivia de Havilland, with John Lund, from *To Each His Own.*

Cinematography: (black and white) Arthur Miller, *Anna and the King of Siam*
(color) Charles Rosher, Leonard Smith, Arthur Arling, *The Yearling*

Editing: Daniel Mandell, *The Best Years of Our Lives*

Original Score: (dramatic or comedy picture) Hugo Friedhofer, *The Best Years of Our Lives*
(musical picture) Morris Stoloff, *The Jolson Story*

Original Song: "On The Atchison, Topeka and Santa Fe," *The Harvey Girls,* Harry Warren, music, Johnny Mercer, lyrics

Art Direction: (black and white) Lyle Wheeler and William Darling, *Anna and the King of Siam*
(color) Cedric Gibbons and Paul Groesse, *The Yearling*

Sound: John Livadary, *The Jolson Story*

Short subjects: (cartoon) "The Cat Concerto" (Tom & Jerry)
(one–reel) "Facing Your Danger"
(two–reel) "A Boy and his Dog"

Documentary: (feature) none nominated
(short) "Seeds of Destiny"

Special Effects: Thomas Howard, *Blithe Spirit*

Thalberg Award: Samuel Goldwyn

Honorary Oscar®: Laurence Olivier, for *Henry V.*
> Harold Russell, for bringing hope and courage to his fellow veterans.
> Ernst Lubitsch.
> Claude Jarman, Jr., outstanding child actor.

Rule Changes: All members of the recognized guilds could continue to nominate their peers, but only members of the Academy were permitted to vote for the awards.

In the '40s, the Academy Awards® became an obsession with producers. Zanuck's *Wilson*, almost everything Selznick produces, and in 1946, Sam Goldwyn's *The Best Years of Our Lives* are films made to win the big awards. An Oscar®-winning profile emerges. An expensive film designed with impeccable mild liberalism that addresses a social problem in such a way that no one could possibly be offended or upset about it, so as not to affect the film's potential earnings. *The Best Years of Our Lives* is almost three hours long, has a director with a sound track record in William Wyler, and says that life is difficult for returning war veterans, which, of course, it is.

Best Years is also the last collaboration of producer Goldwyn and director Wyler. Wyler claimed that Goldwyn had promised to credit the film as "A William Wyler Production," and didn't. For his part, Goldwyn felt it was a personal insult when Wyler formed Liberty Films with George Stevens and Frank Capra. Years later, when an interviewer begins a question "When Wyler made *Wuthering Heights . . .*" Goldwyn will snarl "I made *Wuthering Heights*. Wyler only directed it." And Wyler will in turn ask "What Goldwyn Touch? Name a Goldwyn film that I didn't direct that had 'The Goldwyn Touch.' "

For the first time, Hollywood began to worry about a British invasion—there were eight nominations for British films, and screenplay nominations for *Children of Paradise* and *Open City* (Fellini's first nomination!). If Hollywood of 1946 could have seen the raft of 1992 nominations for *Howard's End*, *The Crying Game*, *Enchanted April* and *Damage*, there would have been collective cardiac arrest.

This year, Billy Wilder presented the directing Oscar® to William Wyler. I'm not the only one who used to confuse the two. After all, they were both European émigrés, they both, late in their careers, won the Thalberg Award, and they won back to back directing Oscars® twice—'45–'46 *(The Lost Weekend/Best Years of Our Lives)* and '59–'60 *(Ben-Hur/The Apartment)*. When Wilder picked up Oscars® for *The Apartment* in '60, Wyler said that he'd be getting a lot of congratulations for them. Like the numerous Franks in the 1930s, Wilder and Wyler only competed once for Best Director, in 1953, when Wyler was nominated for *Roman Holiday* and Wilder for *Stalag 17*.

Fontaine–de Havilland, Round 2: Joan Fontaine went backstage to congratulate her sister on her win, and Olivia de Havilland snubbed her. "Our relations," said de Havilland, "have been strained for some time."

Picture	*The Bishop's Wife*
	Crossfire
	*Gentleman's Agreement
	Great Expectations
	Miracle on 34th Street
Director	George Cukor, *A Double Life*
	Edward Dmytryk, *Crossfire*
	**Elia Kazan, *Gentleman's Agreement*
	Henry Koster, *The Bishop's Wife*
	David Lean, *Great Expectations*
Actor	**Ronald Colman, *A Double Life*
	John Garfield, *Body and Soul*
	Gregory Peck, *Gentleman's Agreement*
	William Powell, *Life with Father*
	Michael Redgrave, *Mourning Becomes Electra*
Actress	Joan Crawford, *Possessed*
	Susan Hayward, *Smash-up—The Story of a Woman*
	Dorothy McGuire, *Gentleman's Agreement*
	Rosalind Russell, *Mourning Becomes Electra*
	**Loretta Young, *The Farmer's Daughter*
Supporting Actor	Charles Bickford, *The Farmer's Daughter*
	Thomas Gomez, *Ride the Pink Horse*
	**Edmund Gwenn, *Miracle on 34th Street*
	Robert Ryan, *Crossfire*
	Richard Widmark, *Kiss of Death*
Supporting Actress	Ethel Barrymore, *The Paradine Case*
	Gloria Grahame, *Crossfire*
	**Celeste Holm, *Gentleman's Agreement*
	Marjorie Main, *The Egg and I*
	Anne Revere, *Gentleman's Agreement*

Original Story: Valentine Davies, *Miracle on 34th Street*

Original Screenplay: Sidney Sheldon, *The Bachelor and the Bobby-Soxer*

Left: Best Actress Loretta Young in *The Farmer's Daughter. Right:* Celeste Holm, Best Supporting Actress for *Gentleman's Agreement.*

Screenplay: George Seaton, *Miracle on 34th Street*

Cinematography: (black and white) Guy Green, *Great Expectations*
(color) Jack Cardiff, *Black Narcissus*

Editing: Francis Lyon and Robert Parrish, *Body and Soul*

Original Score: (dramatic or comedy picture) Miklos Rosza, *A Double Life*
(musical picture) Alfred Newman, *Mother Wore Tights*

Original Song: "Zip–A–Dee–Doo–Dah," *Song of the South,* Allie Wrubel, music, Ray Gilbert, lyrics

Art Direction: (black and white) John Bryan, *Great Expectations*
(color) Alfred Junge, *Black Narcissus*

Sound: *The Bishop's Wife*

Short subjects: (cartoon) "Tweetie Pie" (Merrie Melodies)
(one–reel) "Good–bye Miss Turlock"
(two–reel) "Climbing the Matterhorn"

Documentary: (feature) *Design for Death*
(short) "First Steps"

Special Effects: *Green Dolphin Street,* visual, A. Arnold Gillespie and Warren Newcombe, audible, Douglas Shearer and Michael Steinore

Thalberg Award: Not given

Honorary Oscar®: James Baskette, for his characterization of Uncle Remus.

    Bill and Coo, in which artistry and patience blended in a novel and entertaining use of the medium.

    Shoeshine, for proving that the creative spirit can triumph over adversity.

    Colonel William N. Selig, Albert E. Smith, Thomas Armat and George K. Spoor, motion picture pioneers.

The folks at RKO had a problem at the 1947 Academy Awards®: writer–director Edward Dmytryk and producer Adrian Scott had one of the most acclaimed thrillers of the year in *Crossfire*. Between the completion of the film and the announcement of the Oscar® nominations, Dmytryk and Scott had taken the Fifth before the House Un–American Activities (they were two of the "Unfriendly Ten"), been fired by the studio and effectively blacklisted by the industry's Communist witchhunt. Then they were nominated for Best Picture and Best Director.

While the big awards went roughly as predicted—though Loretta Young's victory in *The Farmer's Daughter* was a surprise—Hollywood was made very nervous by the fact that the British swept the awards for art direction and cinematography (*Great Expectations* taking Black and White Awards, *Black Narcissus* the color) for the first time.

Huh? *The Bachelor and the Bobby–Soxer*, a screenplay by Sidney Sheldon (yes, the best-selling author of *The Other Side of Midnight*) beats out Abraham Polonsky's extraordinary script for *Body and Soul*. I promised not to second-guess the Academy, but this one is too much to let pass without comment.

1948

Picture	*Hamlet* Johnny Belinda The Red Shoes The Snake Pit The Treasure of Sierra Madre
Director	*John Huston, *The Treasure of Sierra Madre* Anatole Litvak, *The Snake Pit* Jean Negulesco, *Johnny Belinda* Laurence Olivier, *Hamlet* Fred Zinneman, *The Search*
Actor	Lew Ayres, *Johnny Belinda* Montgomery Clift, *The Search* Dan Dailey, *When My Baby Smiles at Me* *Laurence Olivier, *Hamlet* Clifton Webb, *Sitting Pretty*
Actress	Ingrid Bergman, *Joan of Arc* Olivia de Havilland, *The Snake Pit* Irene Dunne, *I Remember Mama* Barbara Stanwyck, *Sorry, Wrong Number* *Jane Wyman, *Johnny Belinda*
Supporting Actor	Charles Bickford, *Johnny Belinda* Jose Ferrer, *Joan of Arc* Oscar Homolka, *I Remember Mama* *Walter Huston, *The Treasure of Sierra Madre* Cecil Kellaway, *Luck of the Irish*
Supporting Actress	Barbara Bel Geddes, *I Remember Mama* Ellen Corby, *I Remember Mama* Agnes Moorehead in *Johnny Belinda* Jean Simmons, *Hamlet* *Claire Trevor, *Key Largo*

Motion Picture Story: Richard Schweizer and David Wechsler, *The Search*

Screenplay: John Huston, *The Treasure of Sierra Madre*

Left: 1948, Laurence Olivier, Best Actor/Best Picture *Hamlet. Right:* Jane Wyman, Best Actress in *Johnny Belinda.*

Cinematography: (black and white) William Daniels, *The Naked City*
(color) Joseph Valentine, William V. Skall and Winton Hoch, *Joan of Arc*

Editing: Paul Weatherwax, *The Naked City*

Score: (dramatic or comedy picture) Brian Esdale, *The Red Shoes*
(musical picture) Johnny Green and Roger Edens, *Easter Parade*

Original Song: "Buttons and Bows," *The Paleface,* Jay Livingston and Ray Evans

Art Direction: (black and white) Roger K. Furse, *Hamlet*
Richard Day, *Joan of Arc*

Costume Design: (black and white) Roger K. Furse, *Hamlet*
(color) Dorothy Jeakins and Karinska, *Joan of Arc*

Sound: *The Snake Pit,* 20th Century–Fox Sound Department

Short subjects: (cartoon) "The Little Orphan" (Tom & Jerry)
(one–reel) "Symphony of a City"
(two–reel) "Seal Island"

Documentary: (feature) *The Secret Land*
(short) "Toward Independence"

Special Effects: *Portrait of Jenny,* (visual) Paul Eagler, J. McMillan Johnson, Russell Shearman and Clarence Silver, (sound) Charles Freeman and James G. Stewart

Thalberg Award: Jerry Wald

Honorary Oscar®: *Monsieur Vincent,* outstanding foreign language film.
Ivan Jandl, outstanding juvenile performance *(The Search).*
Sid Grauman, exhibitor.
Adolph Zukor, founder of Paramount.
Walter Wanger, for the production of *Joan of Arc.*

Rule Changes: The category of Costume Design was added, Original Screenplay dropped, and Original Story changed to Motion Picture Story.

The "Paramount decree"—the anti-trust ruling that forced the studios to divest themselves of their theaters—marked the beginning of the end of the studio system that had dominated Hollywood for a quarter century. It is symbolically appropriate that two of the best picture nominations went to foreign films and that the studios themselves decided that they would not underwrite the Oscars®, forcing the Academy to move the Awards show to their own thousand-seat theater.

Although no campaign was mounted for Olivier's *Hamlet,* even after Sir Larry had won the New York Film Critics prize as the best actor, that didn't stop the nominations and another moment of that curious Hollywood schizophrenia that combines rampant Anglophilia with rabid Anglophobia, as *Hamlet* picked up six nominations and *The Red Shoes* grabbed five.

The oddest omission from the nominees was Humphrey Bogart's failure to be nominated for *The Treasure of Sierra Madre,* perhaps the most shocking omission since the Bette Davis/*Of Human Bondage* scandal in 1934. Did Jane Wyman win the Best Actress Oscar® because of her performance in *Johnny Belinda,* or was it a sympathy vote—she'd endured a miscarriage and was in the process of divorcing Ronald Reagan, who joked at the time that he was thinking of naming *Johnny Belinda* as correspondent.

Head Count: Edith Head receives first nomination, for the costume design of *The Emperor Waltz.* Head, a legendary designer who was fond of pointing out that she'd been in Hollywood longer than the Academy Awards®, was one of the few people who seldom said publicly that being nominated was honor enough.

Picture	*All The King's Men*
	Battleground
	The Heiress
	A Letter to Three Wives
	12 O'Clock High
Director	*Joseph L. Mankiewicz, A Letter to Three Wives
	Carol Reed, The Fallen Idol
	Robert Rossen, All the King's Men
	William Wellman, Battleground
	William Wyler, The Heiress
Actor	*Broderick Crawford, All The King's Men
	Kirk Douglas, Champion
	Gregory Peck, 12 O'Clock High
	Richard Todd, The Hasty Heart
	John Wayne, Sands of Iwo Jima
Actress	Jeanne Crain, Pinky
	*Olivia de Havilland, The Heiress
	Susan Hayward, My Foolish Heart
	Deborah Kerr, Edward My Son
	Loretta Young, Come to the Stable
Supporting Actor	John Ireland, All the King's Men
	*Dean Jagger, 12 O'Clock High
	Arthur Kennedy, Champion
	Ralph Richardson, The Heiress
	James Whitmore, Battleground
Supporting Actress	Ethel Barrymore, Pinky
	Celeste Holm, Come to the Stable
	Elsa Lanchester, Come to the Stable
	*Mercedes McCambridge, All the King's Men
	Ethel Waters, Pinky

Motion Picture Story: Douglas Morrow, *The Stratton Story*

Screenplay: Joseph L. Mankiewicz, *A Letter to Three Wives*

Story and Screenplay: Robert Pirosh, *Battleground*

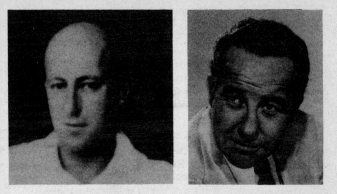

Left: Honorary Oscar® winner Cecil B. DeMille. (crop) *Right:* Best Actor Broderick Crawford in *All the King's Men.*

Cinematography: (black and white) Paul C. Vogel, *Battleground*
(color) Winton Hoch, *She Wore a Yellow Ribbon*

Editing: Harry Gerstad, *Champion*

Score: (dramatic or comedy picture) Aaron Copland, *The Heiress*
(musical picture) Roger Edens and Lennie Hayton, *On The Town*

Original Song: "Baby, It's Cold Outside," *Neptune's Daughter,* Frank Loesser

Art Direction: (black and white) John Meehan, *The Heiress*
(color) Cedric Gibbons and Paul Groesse, *Little Women*

Costume Design: (black and white) Edith Head and Gile Steele, *The Heiress*
(color) Leah Rhodes, Travilla and Marjorie Best, *The Adventures of Don Juan*

Sound: *12 O'Clock High,* 20th Century–Fox Sound Department

Short subjects: (cartoon) "For Scent–imental Reasons" (Merrie Melodies)
(one–reel) "Aquatic House Party"
(two–reel) "Van Gogh"

Documentary: (feature) *Daybreak in Udi*
(short) (two winners) "A Chance to Live"
"So Much For So Little"

Special Effects: *Mighty Joe Young*

Thalberg Award: Not given

Honorary Oscar®: *The Bicycle Thief*, best foreign film.
Bobby Driscoll, outstanding juvenile.
Fred Astaire.
Cecil B. DeMille.
Jean Hersholt, for distinguished service to the industry.

Rule Changes: The Original Screenplay category was revived and
renamed as Story and Screenplay.

Oscar® campaigns are fraught with irony. Darryl F. Zanuck ran
lots of ads for *12 O'Clock High* and none for *A Letter to Three
Wives*. Columbia boss Harry Cohn grudgingly opened *All The
King's Men* but ran no Oscar® campaign for it. *All the King's Men*
got seven nominations, and *A Letter to Three Wives* did better
than *12 O'Clock High*. Go figure. On the other hand, foreign films
were at the very beginning of their post–war runs in America, and
Rossellini's *Paisan* and De Sica's *The Bicycle Thief* were both
nominated for writing awards.

The studios decided to start funding the awards show again,
and Academy president Jean Hersholt got an honorary Oscar® for
his troubles. (Yes, this is the Jean Hersholt the Humanitarian
Award is named for. More on him later.)

A lot of great performances have won Oscars®, but perhaps no
performance is as worthy as Mercedes McCambridge's seventeen
minute debut in *All the King's Men*. Her tough–minded, whiskey-
voiced political operative, aside from being a great performance,
defines what great supporting performances do.

Head Count: Edith Head wins Oscar® for *The Heiress*—second
nomination, first award.

1950

Picture	*All About Eve*
	Born Yesterday
	Father of the Bride
	King Solomon's Mines
	Sunset Boulevard
Director	George Cukor, *Born Yesterday*
	John Huston, *The Asphalt Jungle*
	*Joseph L. Mankiewicz, *All About Eve*
	Carol Reed, *The Third Man*
	Billy Wilder, *Sunset Boulevard*
Actor	Louis Calhern, *The Magnificent Yankee*
	*Jose Ferrer, *Cyrano de Bergerac*
	William Holden, *Sunset Boulevard*
	James Stewart, *Harvey*
	Spencer Tracy, *Father of the Bride*
Actress	Anne Baxter, *All About Eve*
	Bette Davis, *All About Eve*
	*Judy Holliday, *Born Yesterday*
	Eleanor Parker, *Caged*
	Gloria Swanson, *Sunset Boulevard*
Supporting Actor	Jeff Chandler, *Broken Arrow*
	Edmund Gwenn, *Mister 880*
	Sam Jaffe, *The Asphalt Jungle*
	*George Sanders, *All About Eve*
	Erich Von Stroheim, *Sunset Boulevard*
Supporting Actress	Hope Emerson, *Caged*
	Celeste Holm, *All About Eve*
	*Josephine Hull, *Harvey*
	Nancy Olson, *Sunset Boulevard*
	Thelma Ritter, *All About Eve*

Motion Picture Story: Edna and Edward Anhalt, *Panic in the Streets*

Screenplay: Joseph L. Mankiewicz, *All About Eve*

Story and Screenplay: Charles Brackett, Billy Wilder and D.M. Marshman Jr., *Sunset Boulevard*

Cinematography: (black and white) Robert Krasker, *The Third Man*
(color) Robert Surtees, *King Solomon's Mines*

108

Left: Jose Ferrer in *Cyrano de Bergerac. Right:* Best Picture, *All About Eve.*

Editing: Ralph Winters and Conrad A. Nervig, *King Solomon's Mines*

Score: (dramatic or comedy picture) Franz Waxman, *Sunset Boulevard*
(musical picture) Adolph Deutsch and Roger Edens, *Annie Get Your Gun*

Original Song: "Mona Lisa," *Captain Carey*, Ray Evans and Jay Livingston

Art Direction: (black and white) Hans Dreier and John Meehan, *Sunset Boulevard*
(color) Hans Dreier and Walter Tyler, *Samson and Delilah*

Costume Design: (black and white) Edith Head and Charles LeMaire, *All About Eve*
(color) Edith Head, Dorothy Jeakins, Elois Jenssen, Gile Steele and Gwen Wakelling, *Samson and Delilah*

Sound: *All About Eve,* 20th Century–Fox Sound Department

Short subjects: (cartoon) "Gerald McBoing Boing"
(one–reel) "Granddad of Races"
(two–reel) "In Beaver Valley"

Documentary: (feature) *The Titan: Story of Michelangelo*
(short) "Why Korea?"

Special Effects: *Destination Moon*

Thalberg Award: Darryl F. Zanuck

Honorary Oscar®: *The Walls of Malapaga*, outstanding foreign film.
    George Murphy, for services to the industry.
    Louis B. Mayer.

1950's Best Actress race was an interesting case of "what if . . ." While preparing *Sunset Boulevard*, Billy Wilder pitched the role of silent film star Norma Desmond to Mae West, to Mary Pickford (whom he realized, mid–pitch, was all wrong), then to Pola Negri, all of whom turned down the role. George Cukor recommended Gloria Swanson, and the rest, as they say, is history. Coming off his twin Oscars® for writing and directing *A Letter to Three Wives*, Joe Mankiewicz cast Claudette Colbert as aging (fortyish) Broadway star Margo Channing when Colbert suffered a skiing injury and had to drop out, to be replaced by Bette Davis. Harry Cohn bought *Born Yesterday* for Rita Hayworth, but she then quit the movies to marry Aly Khan, leaving the door open for Judy Holliday, who starred in the play on Broadway.

If the theory that roles win Oscars® rather than actors the nominees might have looked like this—

    Anne Baxter, *All About Eve*
    Claudette Colbert, *All About Eve*
    Rita Hayworth, *Born Yesterday*
    Eleanor Parker, *Caged*
    Mae West, *Sunset Boulevard*

—and Anne Baxter probably would have won.

    Marilyn Monroe, then a rising starlet (featured roles in two nominated films, *All About Eve* and *The Asphalt Jungle*), made her one and only Oscar® appearance, presenting the award for Best Sound. One of her directors, Joseph L. Mankiewicz, entered the history books—he became the only person ever to win writing and directing Oscars® in consecutive years.

Head Count: Edith Head wins Oscars® in both the color and black and white categories, for *All About Eve* and *Samson and Delilah*. Second and third Oscars®, third and fourth nominations.

1951

Picture	*An American in Paris*
	Decision Before Dawn
	A Place in the Sun
	Quo Vadis
	A Streetcar Named Desire
Director	John Huston, *The African Queen*
	Elia Kazan, *A Streetcar Named Desire*
	Vincente Minnelli, *An American in Paris*
	*George Stevens, *A Place in the Sun*
	William Wyler, *Detective Story*
Actor	*Humphrey Bogart, *The African Queen*
	Marlon Brando, *A Streetcar Named Desire*
	Montgomery Clift, *A Place in the Sun*
	Arthur Kennedy, *Bright Victory*
	Frederic March, *Death of a Salesman*
Actress	Katharine Hepburn, *The African Queen*
	*Vivien Leigh, *A Streetcar Named Desire*
	Eleanor Parker, *Detective Story*
	Shelley Winters, *A Place in the Sun*
	Jane Wyman, *The Blue Veil*
Supporting Actor	Leo Genn, *Quo Vadis*
	*Karl Malden, *A Streetcar Named Desire*
	Kevin McCarthy, *Death of a Salesman*
	Peter Ustinov, *Quo Vadis*
	Gig Young, *Come Fill The Cup*
Supporting Actress	Joan Blondell, *The Blue Veil*
	Mildred Dunnock, *Death of a Salesman*
	Lee Grant, *Detective Story*
	*Kim Hunter, *A Streetcar Named Desire*
	Thelma Ritter, *The Mating Season*

Motion Picture Story: Paul Dehn and James Bernard, *Seven Days To Noon*

Screenplay: Michael Wilson and Harry Brown, *A Place in the Sun*

Story and Screenplay: Alan Jay Lerner, *An American in Paris*

112

Left: Best Actor Humphrey Bogart, with Katharine Hepburn in *The African Queen. Right:* Best Actress Vivian Leigh, with Marlon Brando in *A Streetcar Named Desire.*

Cinematography: (black and white) William C. Mellor, *A Place in the Sun*

(color) Alfred Gilks and John Alton, *An American in Paris*

Editing: William Hornbeck, *A Place in the Sun*

Score: (dramatic or comedy picture) Franz Waxman, *A Place in the Sun*

(musical picture) Johnny Green and Saul Chaplin, *An American in Paris*

Original Song: "In the Cool, Cool, Cool of the Evening," Hoagy Carmichael, music, Johnny Mercer, lyrics, *Here Comes the Groom*

Art Direction: (black and white) Richard Day, *A Streetcar Named Desire*

(color) Cedric Gibbons and Preston Ames, *An American in Paris*

Costume Design: (black and white) Edith Head, *A Place in the Sun*

(color) Orry-Kelly, Walter Plunkett and Irene Sharaff, *An American in Paris*

Sound: Douglas Shearer, *The Great Caruso*

Short subjects: (cartoon) "Two Mousketeers" (Tom and Jerry)

(one–reel) "World of Kids"
(two–reel) "Nature's Half Acre"

Documentary: (feature) *Kon Tiki*
(short) "Benjy"

Special Effects: *When Worlds Collide*

Thalberg Award: Arthur Freed

Honorary Oscar®: Gene Kelly, for his versatility as actor,
singer, director and dancer.
Rashomon, outstanding foreign film.

Rule Changes: An award for Special Effects would not be given
every year.

"The only honest way to find the best actor would be to let
everybody play Hamlet and let the best man win. Of course,
you'd get some pretty funny Hamlets that way." So spoke Humphrey Bogart, campaigning for his Oscar® nomination for *The
African Queen*. He'd need all the campaigning he could get against
A Streetcar Named Desire, which became the first of only two films
ever to win three acting Oscars®. The only *Streetcar* star not
honored would be Marlon Brando. He would have to wait his
turn, but it was apparently unimportant to him—like most of his
co-stars, he was planning to skip the Awards show. Future Academy president Karl Malden was the only one to show up.
    The Academy decided not to put the program on television
again this year. But the fear of the show running overlong af-
flicted all concerned, and MC Danny Kaye asked that "your
speech be no longer than the movie itself." Good thing no one
from *Quo Vadis* won. On the other hand, the victory of *An American in Paris*—the first musical to win since *Broadway Melody* in
1929—shocked everyone. The smart money was on George Stevens' *A Place in the Sun*. Oddly enough, *An American in Paris*
was also the first color movie to win an Oscar® since *Gone With the
Wind*.

Head Count: Edith Head wins fourth Oscar® (fifth nomination)
for *A Place in the Sun*.

Picture
The Greatest Show on Earth
High Noon
Ivanhoe
Moulin Rouge
The Quiet Man

Director
Cecil B. DeMille, *The Greatest Show On Earth*
* John Ford, *The Quiet Man*
John Huston, *Moulin Rouge*
Joseph L. Mankiewicz, *Five Fingers*
Fred Zinneman, *High Noon*

Actor
Marlon Brando, *Viva Zapata!*
* Gary Cooper, *High Noon*
Kirk Douglas, *The Bad and the Beautiful*
Jose Ferrer, *Moulin Rouge*
Alec Guinness, *The Lavender Hill Mob*

Actress
* Shirley Booth, *Come Back, Little Sheba*
Joan Crawford, *Sudden Fear*
Bette Davis, *The Star*
Julie Harris, *The Member of the Wedding*
Susan Hayward, *With a Song in My Heart*

Supporting Actor
Richard Burton, *My Cousin Rachel*
Arthur Hunnicutt, *The Big Sky*
Victor McLaglen, *The Quiet Man*
Jack Palance, *Sudden Fear*
* Anthony Quinn, *Viva Zapata!*

Supporting Actress
* Gloria Grahame, *The Bad and the Beautiful*
Jean Hagen, *Singin' in the Rain*
Colette Marchand, *Moulin Rouge*
Terry Moore, *Come Back, Little Sheba*
Thelma Ritter, *With a Song in My Heart*

Motion Picture Story: Frederic M. Frank, Theodore St. John, Frank Cavett, *The Greatest Show on Earth*

Left: Gary Cooper, Best Actor in *High Noon*. *Right:* Best Supporting Actor Anthony Quinn in *Viva Zapata!*

Screenplay: Charles M. Schnee, *The Bad and the Beautiful*

Story and Screenplay: T.E.B. Clark, *The Lavender Hill Mob*

Cinematography: (black and white) Robert Surtees, *The Bad and the Beautiful*
(color) Winton Hoch and Archie Stout, *The Quiet Man*

Editing: Elmo Williams and Harry Gerstad, *High Noon*

Score: (musical or dramatic picture) Dimitri Tiomkin, *High Noon*
(musical picture) Alfred Newman, *With a Song in My Heart*

Original Song: "High Noon (Do Not Forsake Me Oh My Darlin')," *High Noon*, Dimitri Tiomkin (music), Ned Washington (lyrics)

Art Direction: (black and white) Cedric Gibbons and Edward Carfagno, *The Bad and the Beautiful*
(color) Paul Sheriff, *Moulin Rouge*

Costume Design: (black and white) Helen Rose, *The Bad and the Beautiful*
(color) Marcel Vertes, *Moulin Rouge*

Sound: *Breaking the Sound Barrier*, London Film Sound Department

Short subjects: (cartoon) "Johann Mouse" (Tom and Jerry)
  (one–reel) "Light in the Window"
  (two–reel) "Water Birds"

Documentary: (feature) *The Sea Around Us*
  (short) "Neighbours"

Special Effects: *Plymouth Adventure*

Thalberg Award: Cecil B. DeMille

Honorary Oscar®: George Alfred Mitchell, for the design of
    the Mitchell Camera.
  Joseph M. Schenck for distinguished service to the
    industry.
  Merion C. Cooper for his innovations and contributions to
    movies.
  Harold Lloyd.
  Bob Hope, for his contribution to the laughter of the
    world.
  Forbidden Games, outstanding foreign film.

1952 marks the beginning of the Oscars® as we know them. That is, live, tacky and right in our living rooms through the miracle of television. It is all the fault of the studios, of course. Warner Brothers, Universal and Columbia announced that they would no longer fund the Awards show, so NBC made an offer for broadcast rights, and Oscar® made his TV debut.

John Wayne accepted Gary Cooper's Oscar® for *High Noon* by making humorous remarks about why his own manager and agent couldn't seem to find him roles as good as *High Noon*—his own performance in *The Quiet Man*, perhaps the finest of his career to that point, hadn't even been nominated, and Wayne would not get another nomination until he proved himself willing to wander into self–parody in *True Grit*.

Shirley Booth displayed an interesting false modesty, noting that it was not fair for her to win, because she'd played her character in *Come Back, Little Sheba*, more than a thousand times. In other words, the competition never had a chance.

Documentary Short winner "Neighbours," a production of Canada's National Film Board from director Norman MacLaren, is not a documentary at all, but a fictional allegory about territorialism and nationalism. It features pixilated motion that treats live actors as figures to be manipulated by the camera. How anyone ever thought it was a documentary remains one of Oscar®'s great mysteries.

Head Count: Edith Head receives sixth and seventh Oscar® nominations for *Carrie* and *The Greatest Show on Earth*. Head also served as fashion consultant to the first televised Oscars® show and got to tell everyone that they shouldn't wear bright white or flaming red because of the rigors of television lighting.

1953

Picture	*From Here to Eternity
	Julius Caesar
	The Robe
	Roman Holiday
	Shane
Director	George Stevens, Shane
	Charles Walters, Lili
	Billy Wilder, Stalag 17
	William Wyler, Roman Holiday
	*Fred Zinneman, From Here to Eternity
Actor	Marlon Brando, Julius Caesar
	Richard Burton, The Robe
	Montgomery Clift, From Here to Eternity
	*William Holden, Stalag 17
	Burt Lancaster, From Here to Eternity
Actress	Leslie Caron, Lili
	Ava Gardner, Mogambo
	*Audrey Hepburn, Roman Holiday
	Deborah Kerr, From Here to Eternity
	Maggie MacNamara, The Moon is Blue
Supporting Actor	Eddie Albert, Roman Holiday
	Brandon De Wilde, Shane
	Jack Palance, Shane
	*Frank Sinatra, From Here to Eternity
	Robert Strauss, Stalag 17
Supporting Actress	Grace Kelly, Mogambo
	Geraldine Page, Hondo
	Marjorie Rambeau, Torch Song
	*Donna Reed, From Here to Eternity
	Thelma Ritter, Pickup On South Street

Motion Picture Story: Ian McLellan Hunter, Roman Holiday

Screenplay: Daniel Taradash, From Here to Eternity

Story and Screenplay: Charles Brackett, Walter Reisch, Richard Breen, Titanic

Cinematography: (black and white) Burnett Guffey, From Here to Eternity
(color) Loyal Griggs, Shane

Left: Donna Reed, Best Supporting Actress, *From Here to Eternity*. *Right:* Audrey Hepburn, Best Actress, *Roman Holiday*.

Editing: William Lyon, *From Here to Eternity*

Score: (dramatic or comedy picture) Bronislau Kaper, *Lili*
(musical picture) Alfred Newman, *Call Me Madam*

Original Song: "Secret Love," *Calamity Jane*, Sammy Fain (music), Paul Francis Webster (lyrics)

Art Direction: (black and white) Cedric Gibbons and Edward Carfagno, *Julius Caesar*
(color) Lyle Wheeler and George W. Davis, *The Robe*

Costume Design: (black and white) Edith Head, *Roman Holiday*
Charles LeMaire and Emile Santiago, *The Robe*

Sound: John P. Livadary, Columbia Sound Department, *From Here to Eternity*

Short subjects: (cartoon) "Toot, Whistle Plunk and Boom" (Disney)
(one–reel) "The Merry Wives of Windsor Overture"
(two–reel) "Bear Country"

Documentary: (feature) *The Living Desert*
(short) "The Alaskan Eskimo"

Special Effects: *War of the Worlds*

Thalberg Award: George Stevens

Honorary Oscar®: Pete Smith, for his witty short films.
 20th Century–Fox, for introducing CinemaScope.
 Joseph Breen, for managing the Motion Picture Code
  (head censor).
 Bell and Howell.

There were problems with the writing category. Louis L'Amour was nominated for best original screenplay for John Wayne's 3–D Western, *Hondo*. L'Amour felt compelled to point out to the Academy that while he appreciated the nomination, the script was based on a short story that he'd written some years before. Ian McClellan Hunter, who won Motion Picture Story for *Roman Holiday*, was dodging House Un–American Activities Committee subpoenas, had been hiding out in Mexico. Better still, Hunter was a front for Dalton Trumbo, one of the original Unfriendly Ten.

Blacklisted and nominated: According to Billy Wilder, "Only three of the Unfriendly Ten had any talent. The rest were just unfriendly." The following writers were both blacklisted for their Communist associations at some point during the period between 1947 and 1960 and nominated for Oscars®, sometimes simultaneously.

 1940—Dalton Trumbo, *Kitty Foyle*
 1941—Lillian Hellman, *The Little Foxes*
 *1942—Ring Lardner Jr., *Woman of the Year*
 1943—Lillian Hellman, *The North Star*
    Allan Scott, *So Proudly We Hail*
    Hellman and Dashiel Hammett, *Watch on the
    Rhine*
 1945—Alvah Bessie, *Objective, Burma*
    Albert Maltz, *Pride of the Marines*
 1947—Adrian Scott (producer), Edward Dmytryk
    (director), *Crossfire*
    Abraham Polonsky, *Body and Soul*
 1949—Carl Foreman, *Champion*
    Robert Rossen (writer & director), *All The King's
    Men*
 1950—Ben Maddow, *The Asphalt Jungle*
    Carl Foreman, *The Men*
 *1951—Michael Wilson, *A Place in the Sun*
 1952—Michael Wilson, *Five Fingers*
    Carl Foreman, *High Noon*
 *1953—Ian McLellan Hunter/Dalton Trumbo, *Roman
    Holiday*

   *1956—Dalton Trumbo (as Robert Rich), *The Brave One*
          Michael Wilson, *Friendly Persuasion*
   *1957—Carl Foreman and Michael Wilson, *The Bridge on
          the River Kwai*
   *1958—Ned Young (Nathan E. Douglas) *The Defiant Ones*
    1960—Nathan Douglas, *Inherit the Wind*
          Jules Dassin (writer–director), *Never on Sunday*
    1961—Carl Foreman, *The Guns of Navarone*
   *1969—Waldo Salt, *Midnight Cowboy*
   *1970—Ring Lardner, Jr., *M*A*S*H**
    1972—Carl Foreman, *Young Winston*
    1973—Waldo Salt, *Serpico*

(*Oscar® winner)

Head Count: Edith Head wins fifth Costume Design Oscar® (eighth nomination) for *Roman Holiday*.

Picture	*The Caine Mutiny*
	The Country Girl
	On the Waterfront
	Seven Brides for Seven Brothers
	Three Coins in the Fountain
Director	Alfred Hitchcock, *Rear Window*
	*Elia Kazan, *On the Waterfront*
	George Seaton, *The Country Girl*
	William Wellman, *The High and the Mighty*
	Billy Wilder, *Sabrina*
Actor	Humphrey Bogart, *The Caine Mutiny*
	*Marlon Brando, *On the Waterfront*
	Bing Crosby, *The Country Girl*
	James Mason, *A Star is Born*
	Dan O'Herlihy, *The Adventures of Robinson Crusoe*
Actress	Dorothy Dandridge, *Carmen Jones*
	Judy Garland, *A Star is Born*
	Audrey Hepburn, *Sabrina*
	*Grace Kelly, *The Country Girl*
	Jane Wyman, *Magnificent Obsession*
Supporting Actor	Lee J. Cobb, *On the Waterfront*
	Karl Malden, *On the Waterfront*
	*Edmond O'Brien, *The Barefoot Contessa*
	Rod Steiger, *On the Waterfront*
	Tom Tully, *The Caine Mutiny*
Supporting Actress	Nina Foch, *Executive Suite*
	Katy Jurado, *Broken Lance*
	*Eva Marie Saint, *On the Waterfront*
	Jan Sterling, *The High and the Mighty*
	Claire Trevor, *The High and the Mighty*

Motion Picture Story: Philip Yordan, *Broken Lance*

Screenplay: George Seaton, *The Country Girl*

Story and Screenplay: Budd Schulberg, *On the Waterfront*

Left: Best Actor Marlon Brando in Best Picture, *On The Waterfront*. *Right:* Grace Kelly, Best Actress, *The Country Girl*.

Cinematography (black and white): Boris Kaufman, *On the Waterfront*
   (color): Milton Krasner, *Three Coins in the Fountain*

Editing: Gene Milford, *On the Waterfront*

Score: (drama or comedy) Dimitri Tiomkin, *The High and the Mighty*
   (musical) Adolph Deutsch and Saul Chaplin, *Seven Brides for Seven Brothers*

Original Song: "Three Coins in the Fountain," *Three Coins in the Fountain*, Jule Styne (music), Sammy Cahn (lyrics)

Art Direction: (black and white) Richard Day, *On the Waterfront*
   (color) John Meehan, *20,000 Leagues Under the Sea*

Costume Design: (black and white) Edith Head, *Sabrina*
   (color) Sanzo Wada, *Gate of Hell*

Sound: Leslie I. Carey, *The Glenn Miller Story*

Short subjects: (cartoon) "When Magoo Flew"
   (one–reel) "This Mechanical Age"
   (two–reel) "A Time Out of War"

Documentary: (feature) *The Vanishing Prairie*
   (short) "Thursday's Children"

Special Effects: *20,000 Leagues Under the Sea*

Thalberg Award: Not given

Honorary Oscar®: Bausch and Lomb.
Kemp R. Niver for contributions to film restoration.
Greta Garbo.
Danny Kaye for his talent, service to the Academy and
industry.
Jon Whitely, outstanding juvenile, *The Little Kidnappers*.
Vincent Winter, outstanding performance, *The Little
Kidnappers*.
Gate of Hell, best foreign film.

There's a bizarre irony that the one great film to emerge from the
blacklist was a study of the morality of informing, created by two
men who had "named names" to the House Un–American Activities Committee. Director Elia Kazan and Budd Schulberg joined
forces to create *On the Waterfront*. It was important in more ways
than one. Producer Sam Spiegel listed leading lady Eva Marie
Saint as a supporting actress. Her precedent setting nomination
and victory paved the way for Goldie Hawn, Geena Davis,
Marisa Tomei and Jessica Lange.

1954 also saw one of the most famous best actress duels, between Grace Kelly as the wife of an alcoholic in *The Country Girl*
versus Judy Garland's comeback as the wife of an alcoholic in *A
Star is Born*, Garland's only film between *Summer Stock* in 1950
and *A Judgment at Nuremberg* in 1961. If Garland was coming
back, Kelly was saying "Hello, I must be going"—a year later,
she would be on her way to Monaco. Garland also provided one
of those sickroom vigils the Academy is so fond of—she was ex-
pecting her third child immediately.

Oscar® Trivia: Garland was playing the same character—Esther
Blodgett/Vicki Lester/Mrs. Norman Maine that had gotten Janet
Gaynor a nomination in the 1937, non–musical version of *A Star
is Born*. Surprisingly, there are several instances of actors nominated for playing the same character in different movies:

The Letter: Jeanne Eagels (1928–29), Bette Davis (1940).
Henry V: Laurence Olivier (1944) and Kenneth Branagh
(1989)—both also nominated for directing.
Henry VIII: Charles Laughton (*The Private Life of . . . ,*
1932–33), Robert Shaw (*A Man For All Seasons*, 1966)
and Richard Burton (*Anne of the Thousand Days*, 1969).
Norman Maine: Fredric March (1937) and James Mason
(1954).
Professor Henry Higgins: Leslie Howard (*Pygmalion*) and
Rex Harrison (*My Fair Lady*).

130

Mr. Chips: Robert Donat *(Goodbye, Mr. Chips,* 1939) and Peter O'Toole (1969).

"Joe," the boxer/football player: Robert Montgomery *(Here Comes Mr. Jordan,* 1941), Warren Beatty *(Heaven Can Wait,* 1978)

"Max," Joe's trainer: James Gleason *(Mr. Jordan)*, Jack Warden *(Heaven Can Wait)*.

The father in *The Yearling:* Gregory Peck (1946), Rip Torn plays the character who inspired Marjorie Kinnon Rawlings to write *The Yearling* in *Cross Creek* (1983).

Cyrano de Bergerac: Jose Ferrer (1950) and Gerard Depardieu (1990).

Vito Corleone: Marlon Brando *(The Godfather,* 1972) and Robert DeNiro *(Godfather II,* 1974) are the only actors to win Oscars® for playing the same character.

Hyman Roth/Meyer Lansky: Lee Strasberg *(Godfather II,* 1974) and Ben Kingsley *(Bugsy,* 1991).

Rose: Kate Winslet/Gloria Stuart in *Titanic* (1997).

And, of course, Bing Crosby was nominated twice for playing the priest in *Going My Way* and *The Bells of St. Mary's,* Paul Newman was nominated twice as Fast Eddie Felson in *The Hustler* and *The Color of Money,* and Al Pacino was nominated three times for Michael Corleone in *The Godfather* films. Then there's the oddity of Peter Sellers' nomination for *Doctor Strangelove*—three different characters, one nomination.

Head Count: Edith Head wins sixth Oscar® for *Sabrina* (ninth nomination).

1955

Picture	*Love Is a Many–Splendored Thing*
	* *Marty*
	Mister Roberts
	Picnic
	The Rose Tattoo
Director	Elia Kazan, *East of Eden*
	David Lean, *Summertime*
	Joshua Logan, *Picnic*
	*Delbert Mann, *Marty*
	John Sturges, *Bad Day at Black Rock*
Actor	*Ernest Borgnine, *Marty*
	James Cagney, *Love Me Or Leave Me*
	James Dean, *East of Eden*
	Frank Sinatra, *The Man With the Golden Arm*
	Spencer Tracy, *Bad Day at Black Rock*
Actress	Susan Hayward, *I'll Cry Tomorrow*
	Katharine Hepburn, *Summertime*
	Jennifer Jones, *Love Is a Many–Splendored Thing*
	*Anna Magnani, *The Rose Tattoo*
	Eleanor Parker, *Interrupted Melody*
Supporting Actor	Arthur Kennedy, *Trial*
	*Jack Lemmon, *Mister Roberts*
	Joe Mantell, *Marty*
	Sal Mineo, *Rebel Without a Cause*
	Arthur O'Connell, *Picnic*
Supporting Actress	Betsy Blair, *Marty*
	Peggy Lee, *Pete Kelly's Blues*
	Marisa Pavan, *The Rose Tattoo*
	*Jo Van Fleet, *East of Eden*
	Natalie Wood, *Rebel Without a Cause*

Motion Picture Story: Daniel Fuchs, *Love Me Or Leave Me*

Screenplay: Paddy Chayefsky, *Marty*

Story and Screenplay: William Ludwig and Sonya Levien, *Interrupted Melody*

Left: Anna Magnani, Best Actress, *The Rose Tattoo. Right:* Ernest Borgnine, Best Actor, in *Marty.*

Cinematography: (black and white) James Wong Howe, *The Rose Tattoo*
(color) Robert Burks, *To Catch a Thief*

Editing: Charles Nelson and William A. Lyon, *Picnic*

Score: (dramatic or comedy film) Alfred Newman, *Love Is a Many–Splendored Thing*
(musical picture) Robert Russell Bennett, Jay Blackton and Adolph Deutsch, *Oklahoma!*

Original Song: "Love Is a Many–Splendored Thing," *Love Is a Many–Splendored Thing,* Sammy Fain, music, Paul Francis Webster, lyrics

Art Direction: (black and white) Hal Pereira and Tambi Larsen, *The Rose Tattoo*
(color) William Flannery and Jo Mielziner, *Picnic*

Costume Design: (black and white) Helen Rose, *I'll Cry Tomorrow*
(color) Charles LeMaire, *Love Is a Many–Splendored Thing*

Sound: Fred Hynes, Todd-AO Sound Department, *Oklahoma!*

Short subjects: (cartoon) "Speedy Gonzales"
(one–reel) "Survival City"
(two–reel) "The Face of Lincoln"

Documentary: (feature) *Helen Keller in Her Story*
(short) "Men Against the Arctic"

Special Effects: *The Bridges at Toko–Ri*

Thalberg Award: Not given

Honorary Oscar®: *Samurai, The Legend of Musahi,* best foreign film.

There is a feeling among Academy voters that the Oscars® should be everything to everybody, so one often finds them swinging from honoring expensive mega–productions to thinking small. The '50s are an epic period for the Oscars®: *From Here To Eternity, Around the World in 80 Days, Ben Hur, The Ten Commandments.* Hammocked in the middle of the decade are the modest *On the Waterfront,* which cost less than a million and *Marty,* a film so inexpensive that the producers spent more on its Oscar® campaign than they spent making the film. *Marty* also has the historical distinction of being the first film to win both the Oscar® for Best Picture and the Palme D'Or as Best Film at the Cannes Film Festival.

Jerry Lewis hosted the Awards Show for the first time, and the television show became increasingly elaborate and international: Audrey Hepburn presented Best Picture on film from London and Marlon Brando, in Manila, read the Best Actress nominations, and there was again a wing of the show broadcast from NBC in New York.

Interrupted Melody won story and screenplay—what we now think of as Original Screenplay—despite being based on the autobiography of opera singer Marjorie Lawrence.

Head Count: Alert the media—Edith Head failed to win an Oscar® this year, but has 10th and 11th nominations for *The Rose Tattoo* and *To Catch a Thief.* On the other hand, when your job is putting clothes on Grace Kelly and Audrey Hepburn, how can you look bad? Head describes the loss to *Love Is a Many–Splendored Thing* as the greatest disappointment of her career.

1956

Picture	*Around the World in 80 Days*
	Friendly Persuasion
	Giant
	The King and I
	The Ten Commandments
Director	Michael Anderson, *Around the World in 80 Days*
	Walter Lang, *The King and I*
	*George Stevens, *Giant*
	King Vidor, *War and Peace*
	William Wyler, *Friendly Persuasion*
Actor	*Yul Brynner, *The King and I*
	James Dean, *Giant*
	Kirk Douglas, *Lust for Life*
	Rock Hudson, *Giant*
	Laurence Olivier, *Richard III*
Actress	Carroll Baker, *Baby Doll*
	*Ingrid Bergman, *Anastasia*
	Katharine Hepburn, *The Rainmaker*
	Nancy Kelly, *The Bad Seed*
	Deborah Kerr, *The King and I*
Supporting Actor	Don Murray, *Bus Stop*
	Anthony Perkins, *Friendly Persuasion*
	*Anthony Quinn, *Lust for Life*
	Mickey Rooney, *The Bold and the Brave*
	Robert Stack, *Written on the Wind*
Supporting Actress	Mildred Dunnock, *Baby Doll*
	Eileen Heckart, *The Bad Seed*
	Mercedes McCambridge, *Giant*
	Patty McCormack, *The Bad Seed*
	*Dorothy Malone, *Written on the Wind*

Motion Picture Story: Robert Rich (Dalton Trumbo), *The Brave One*

Original Screenplay: Albert Lamorisse, *The Red Balloon*

Adapted Screenplay: James Poe, John Farrow and S.J. Perelman, *Around the World in 80 Days*

Left: Ingrid Bergman, Best Actress, *Anastasia*. *Right:* Robert Newton and David Niven in the Best Picture winner, *Around the World in 80 Days*.

Foreign Film: *La Strada*, Italy, Federico Fellini

Cinematography: (black and white) Joseph Ruttenberg, *Somebody Up There Likes Me*
(color) Lionel Lindon, *Around the World in 80 Days*

Editing: Gene Ruggiero and Paul Weatherwax, *Around the World in 80 Days*

Score: (dramatic or comedy picture) Victor Young, *Around the World in 80 Days*
(musical) Alfred Newman and Ken Darby, *The King and I*

Original Song: "Que Sera, Sera," *The Man Who Knew Too Much*, Jay Livingston and Ray Evans

Art Direction: (black and white) Cedric Gibbons and Malcolm F. Brown, *Somebody Up There Likes Me*
(color) Lyle R. Wheeler and John DeCuir, *The King and I*

Costume Design: (black and white) Jean-Louis, *The Solid Gold Cadillac*
(color) Irene Sharaff, *The King and I*

Sound: Carl Faulkner, 20th Century–Fox Studio Sound Department, *The King and I*

Short subjects: (cartoon) "Mister Magoo's Puddle Jumper"
(one–reel) "Crashing the Water Barrier"
(two–reel) "The Bespoke Overcoat"

Documentary: (feature) *The Silent World* (Jacques Cousteau) (short) "The True Story of the Civil War"

Special Effects: John Fulton, *The Ten Commandments*

Thalberg Award: Buddy Adler

Jean Hersholt Humanitarian Award: Y. Frank Freeman

Honorary Oscar®: Eddie Cantor, for service to the film industry.

After much singularly morbid consideration, I have decided that 1956 was the worst year for the Oscars®. Of the five best picture nominees, only *The Ten Commandments* and *Giant* even survive in filmgoers' memories, the former as a perennial Holy Week/Passover TV special, the latter as the last and least essential piece of the James Dean filmography. *The King And I? Friendly Persuasion? Around The World In 80 Days?* Yul Brynner as Best Actor? Ingrid Bergman's turgid return in *Anastasia* for Best Actress?

1956 was an excellent year for American movies: John Ford's *The Searchers*, Alfred Hitchcock's *The Wrong Man*, Nicholas Ray's *Bigger Than Life, Invasion of the Body Snatchers*, Kirk Douglas' tortured performance as Vincent Van Gogh in *Lust for Life*. But except for Douglas, none of them were even nominated.

The fun was with the writing nominations. The musical *High Society* received an original screenplay nomination, even though it was an adaptation of *The Philadelphia Story* (that is, a musical adaptation of a movie based on a play). Furthermore, the writers nominated—Elwood Ullman and Edward Bernds—didn't write the movie, though they had written a Bowery Boys comedy with the same title. Then *Friendly Persuasion* was nominated as Best Adapted screenplay, only the blacklisted Michael Wilson was the author of the script, and the Academy decided that it would be impolitic to violate the blacklist, so people who had taken the Fifth before a congressional committee were declared ineligible. The Writers' Guild, which was not informed of these changes, was not amused.

Best of all, the Motion Picture Story prize was given to "Robert Rich" for *The Brave One*. Rich turned out to be the blacklisted Dalton Trumbo. The best original screenplay award went to *The Red Balloon*—a film without dialogue.

Who the hell was Jean Hersholt? The Jean Hersholt Humanitarian Award was created, and named after past Academy president and actor Jean Hersholt. Who? Hersholt was never a star—his biggest roles were as the sheriff who ends up handcuffed to Gowland Gibson in Von Stroheim's *Greed* and as the doorman whose wife is in labor in *Grand Hotel*. He worked extensively for charitable endeavors and served as Academy president in the late '40s and early '50s, overseeing the Academy Awards® transformation into a television spectacle and keeping the show afloat when the studios wanted to cut funding.

Much is made of the many nominations without a win for Richard Burton, Peter O'Toole, and Thelma Ritter. Composer Victor Young had more nominations than those three *combined* before he won his first Oscar®. *The Turning Point* and *The Color Purple* are the films to get the most Oscar® nominations without winning—11 apiece. Young had as many nominations as *The Turning Point* and *The Color Purple* combined, most notably for the song *My Foolish Heart* and the scores for *Hold Back the Dawn* and *For Whom the Bell Tolls*. His finest score, for *The Uninvited*, was not nominated. In 1956, he won for *Around the World in 80 Days*. He died before the ceremony.

Rule Changes: No Communists were allowed to win awards. Story and Screenplay became Screenplay—Original. Screenplay became Adapted Screenplay. Foreign Film was now a competitive category, not a committee award. Jean Hersholt Humanitarian Award created.

Head Count: Twelve and unlucky thirteen—Edith Head nominated for *The Proud and the Profane*, and as part of the team that designed costumes for *The Ten Commandments*.

1957

Picture	*The Bridge on the River Kwai* (starred)

Picture   **The Bridge on the River Kwai*
                 Peyton Place
                 Sayonara
                 12 Angry Men
                 Witness For the Prosecution

Director   *David Lean, *The Bridge on the River Kwai*
                 Joshua Logan, *Sayonara*
                 Sidney Lumet, *12 Angry Men*
                 Mark Robson, *Peyton Place*
                 Billy Wilder, *Witness For the Prosecution*

Actor   Marlon Brando, *Sayonara*
                 Anthony Franciosa, *A Hatful of Rain*
                *Alec Guinness, *The Bridge on the River Kwai*
                 Charles Laughton, *Witness For the Prosecution*
                 Anthony Quinn, *Wild is the Wind*

Actress   Deborah Kerr, *Heaven Knows, Mr. Allison*
                 Anna Magnani, *Wild is the Wind*
                 Elizabeth Taylor, *Raintree County*
                 Lana Turner, *Peyton Place*
                *Joanne Woodward, *The Three Faces of Eve*

Supporting Actor   *Red Buttons, *Sayonara*
                 Vittorio de Sica, *A Farewell to Arms*
                 Sessu Hayakawa, *The Bridge on the River Kwai*
                 Arthur Kennedy, *Peyton Place*
                 Russ Tamblyn, *Peyton Place*

Supporting Actress   Carolyn Jones, *The Bachelor Party*
                 Elsa Lanchester, *Witness For the Prosecution*
                 Hope Lange, *Peyton Place*
                *Miyoshi Umeki, *Sayonara*
                 Diane Varsi, *Peyton Place*

Left: William Holden with Best Actor winner Alec Guinness in *The Bridge on the River Kwai*. *Right:* Joanne Woodward, Best Supporting Actress in *The Three Faces of Eve*.

Original Screenplay: George Wells, *Designing Woman*

Adapted Screenplay: Pierre Boulle, *The Bridge on the River Kwai*, Michael Wilson and Carl Foreman (See Blacklisted and Nominated, page 124.)

Foreign Film: *The Nights of Cabiria*, Italy, Federico Fellini

Cinematography: Jack Hildyard, *The Bridge on the River Kwai*

Editing: Peter Taylor, *The Bridge on the River Kwai*

Score: Malcolm Arnold, *The Bridge on the River Kwai*

Original Song: "All the Way," *The Joker is Wild*, James Van Heusen (music), Sammy Cahn (lyrics)

Art Direction: Ted Haworth, *Sayonara*

Costume Design: Orry–Kelly, *Les Girls*

Sound: George Groves, Warner Brothers Sound Department, *Sayonara*

Short subjects: (cartoon) "Birds Anonymous" (live action) "The Wetback Hound"

Documentary: (feature) *Albert Schweitzer* (short) none nominated

Special Effects: Walter Rossi, *The Enemy Below*

Thalberg Award: Not given

Jean Hersholt Humanitarian Award: Samuel Goldwyn

Honorary Oscar®: Charles Brackett for service to the Academy.

B.H. Kahane, for service to the industry.

Gilbert "Bronco Billy" Anderson, for his contributions to the development of motion pictures as entertainment.

The Society of Motion Picture and Television Engineers.

Rule Changes: The nomination procedures change. Formerly, members of the guilds nominated, and members of the Academy voted. As of this year, only Academy members are allowed to nominate and vote. Cinematography, Art Direction, Costume Design eliminate split between black and white and color. Short subjects combine one- and two-reel categories into single category. Screenwriting split into two categories: Screenplay—based on material from another medium, and Screenplay—written directly for the screen. The Academy Awards® take the form by which we know them today.

Myoshi Umecki became the first Asian actress to win an Oscar®, for her performance in *Sayonara*, and one of the few performers to win an Oscar® for her film debut. There are many stories of how one couple in a household winning an Oscar® and the award doing irreparable damage, or making a bad situation worse, but that plainly was not true at Paul Newman's house—Mrs. Newman, Joanne Woodward, won hers for *The Three Faces of Eve* in 1957. Paul would not win his for another 30 years.

In 1947, when Jane Wyman and Ronald Reagan divorced, Reagan had joked about naming Wyman's Oscar® vehicle, *Johnny Belinda*. Ten years later, British actress Ann Todd divorced director David Lean on grounds of desertion—he'd spent months in Ceylon making *The Bridge on the River Kwai*, producer Sam Spiegel's second great Oscar® winner.

The sweep for *River Kwai* led to another blacklisting controversy. Pierre Boulle, the author of the book from which the film was adapted, won the Adapted Screenplay award. There were a couple of problems with this. The first was that Boulle didn't write in English, as hard as it may be to imagine his novel *Planet of the Apes* in French. The second was that the actual writing was done by our old friends, Carl Foreman and the ubiquitous Michael Wilson. (The problem with Wilson was that blacklist or no, he was too good a screenwriter for people to leave alone.) Foreman and Wilson never got their Oscars®, though the Academy decided in 1985 that it was all right to acknowledge them, and the writers' widows received the statuettes.

The trashiest behavior around the Oscars® involved Best Actress nominee Lana Turner *(Peyton Place)* and her boyfriend, mobster Johnny Stompanato. When Turner didn't take Stompanato to the Awards as her date, he waited at her house and beat her when she got home. Ten days later, Stompanato was dead, and Turner's daughter Cheryl (who had gone to the Oscars® with her mother) was charged with the murder and acquitted. Woody Allen, of all people, would take this as the underlying event between the mother and daughter characters in *September*, one of his lesser films.

Head Count: . . . and *Funny Face* makes it fourteen.

Picture	*Auntie Mame*
	Cat on a Hot Tin Roof
	The Defiant Ones
	*Gigi
	Separate Tables
Director	Richard Brooks, *Cat on a Hot Tin Roof*
	Stanley Kramer, *The Defiant Ones*
	*Vincente Minnelli, *Gigi*
	Mark Robson, *Inn of the Sixth Happiness*
	Robert Wise, *I Want To Live*
Actor	Tony Curtis, *The Defiant Ones*
	Paul Newman, *Cat on a Hot Tin Roof*
	*David Niven, *Separate Tables*
	Sidney Poitier, *The Defiant Ones*
	Spencer Tracy, *The Old Man and the Sea*
Actress	*Susan Hayward, *I Want to Live!*
	Deborah Kerr, *Separate Tables*
	Shirley MacLaine, *Some Came Running*
	Rosalind Russell, *Auntie Mame*
	Elizabeth Taylor, *Cat on a Hot Tin Roof*
Supporting Actor	Theodore Bikel, *The Defiant Ones*
	Lee J. Cobb, *The Brothers Karamazov*
	*Burl Ives, *The Big Country*
	Arthur Kennedy, *Some Came Running*
	Gig Young, *Teacher's Pet*
Supporting Actress	Peggy Cass, *Auntie Mame*
	*Wendy Hiller, *Separate Tables*
	Martha Hyder, *Some Came Running*
	Maureen Stapleton, *Lonelyhearts*
	Cara Williams, *The Defiant Ones*

Original Screenplay: Nathan E. Douglas and Harold Jacob Smith, *The Defiant Ones*

Adapted Screenplay: Alan Jay Lerner, *Gigi*

Foreign Film: *Mon Oncle*, France, Jacques Tati

Left: Leslie Caron and Louis Jourdan in Best Picture, *Gigi*. *Right:* Best Actress Susan Hayward in *I Want to Live*.

Cinematography: (color) Joseph Ruttenberg, *Gigi*
(black and white) Sam Leavitt, *The Defiant Ones*

Editing: Adrienne Fazan, *Gigi*

Score: (dramatic or comedy picture) Dimitri Tiomkin, *The Old Man and the Sea*
(musical) Andre Previn, *Gigi*

Original Song: "Gigi," *Gigi*, Frederick Loewe (music), Alan Jay Lerner (lyrics)

Art Direction: William Horning and Preston Ames, *Gigi*

Costume Design: Cecil Beaton, *Gigi*

Sound: Fred Hynes, Todd-AO Sound Dept., *South Pacific*

Short subjects: (cartoon) "Knighty Knight, Bugs"
(live action) "Grand Canyon"

Documentary: (feature) *White Wilderness*
(short) "AMA Girls"

Thalberg Award: Jack L. Warner

Jean Hersholt Humanitarian Award: Not given this year

Honorary Oscar®: Maurice Chevalier.

Rule Changes: Cinematography and Scoring both split—back to black and white/color for the former, musical and non–musical pictures for the latter. Once again, Communists are allowed to win Oscars®. The Academy decides that if the writers are going to continue to nominate them, they might as well be allowed to compete.

The 1958 Oscars® are legendary, less for the *Gigi* sweep than because the producer of the show, Jerry Wald, was so dedicated to bringing the show in on time—cutting monologues and musical numbers as the show was in progress—that after the presentation of the best picture award finale, MC Jerry Lewis was told that he had to fill 20 minutes. He could not.

The victory of *Gigi* leads to a couple of interesting thoughts on the Academy Awards®, musicals and their directors. Vincente Minnelli was the great stylist of the MGM musical—*The Pirate, Meet Me in St. Louis, The Band Wagon, An American in Paris*. He was also one of their finest directors of melodrama—*The Bad and the Beautiful* and *Some Came Running*. Yet Minnelli, like George Cukor on *My Fair Lady* six years later, would be honored for a film that played away from his greatest strengths. Both were delicate directors dealing with earthbound material, both were miniaturists (look at *Meet Me in St. Louis*—it's as exquisitely wrought as any cameo brooch). One wonders if the preponderance of directors who win for big, logistically challenging films is a reflection of Hollywood's view of the director. Less an artist than, in Sydney Pollack's phrase, "a damage containment expert." While actors and actresses are often honored for their best work, directors almost never are—Kazan's Oscar® for *On the Waterfront* and Mankiewicz's for *All About Eve* notwithstanding. None of John Ford's six Oscars® are for his Westerns, which are the soul of his body of work.

On a more serious note, Bugs Bunny finally won his first Oscar® in 1958.

Head Count: Though she can't beat the momentum of the *Gigi* sweep, Edith Head gets fifteenth nomination for *The Buccaneer*.

1959

Picture	*Anatomy of a Murder*
	* *Ben-Hur*
	The Diary of Anne Frank
	The Nun's Story
	Room at the Top
Director	Jack Clayton, *Room at the Top*
	George Stevens, *The Diary of Anne Frank*
	Billy Wilder, *Some Like It Hot*
	* William Wyler, *Ben-Hur*
	Fred Zinneman, *The Nun's Story*
Actor	Laurence Harvey, *Room at the Top*
	* Charlton Heston, *Ben-Hur*
	Jack Lemmon, *Some Like It Hot*
	Paul Muni, *The Last Angry Man*
	James Stewart, *Anatomy of a Murder*
Actress	Doris Day, *Pillow Talk*
	Audrey Hepburn, *The Nun's Story*
	Katharine Hepburn, *Suddenly, Last Summer*
	* Simone Signoret, *Room at the Top*
	Elizabeth Taylor, *Suddenly, Last Summer*
Supporting Actor	*Hugh Griffith, *Ben-Hur*
	Arthur O'Connell, *Anatomy of a Murder*
	George C. Scott, *Anatomy of a Murder*
	Robert Vaughan, *The Young Philadelphians*
	Ed Wynn, *The Diary of Anne Frank*
Supporting Actress	Hermione Baddely, *Room at the Top*
	Susan Kohner, *Imitation of Life*
	Juanita Moore, *Imitation of Life*
	Thelma Ritter, *Pillow Talk*
	* Shelley Winters, *The Diary of Anne Frank*

Original Screenplay: Russell Rouse and Clarence Greene, Stanley Shapiro and Maurice Richlin, *Pillow Talk*

Left: Shelly Winters, Best Supporting Actress, *Diary of Anne Frank. Right:* Honorary Oscar® winner Buster Keaton.

Adapted Screenplay: Neil Paterson, *Room at the Top*

Foreign Film: *Black Orpheus,* French, Marcel Camus

Cinematography: (black and white) William C. Mellor, *The Diary of Anne Frank*
(color) Robert L. Surtees, *Ben–Hur*

Editing: Ralph E. Winters and John Dunning, *Ben–Hur*

Score: (drama or comedy) Miklos Rosza, *Ben–Hur*
(musical) Andre Previn and Ken Darby, *Porgy and Bess*

Original Song: "High Hopes," *A Hole in the Head,* James Van Heusen (music), Sammy Cahn (lyrics)

Art Direction: (black and white) Lyle R. Wheeler and George W. Davis, *The Diary of Anne Frank*
(color) William A. Horning and Edward Carfagno, Hugh Hunt, *Ben–Hur*

Costume Design: (black and white) Orry–Kelly, *Some Like It Hot*
(color) Elizabeth Haffenden, *Ben–Hur*

Sound: Franklin E. Milton, MGM Sound Dept., *Ben–Hur*

Short subjects: (cartoon) "Moonbird"
(live action) "The Golden Fish"

Documentary: (feature) *Serengeti Shall Not Die*
(short) "Glass"

Special Effects: Arnold Gillespie and Robert MacDonald (visual), Milor Lory (audio), *Ben-Hur*

Thalberg Award: Not given

Jean Hersholt Humanitarian Award: Bob Hope

Honorary Oscar®: Buster Keaton.
Lee de Forest, for the development of sound.

Rule Changes: Art Direction and Costume Design re–split their awards into black and white and color.

"Hollywood," said Shirley Knight, "is where they give Charlton Heston awards for acting." Which is rather unfair, because Heston is a very good actor. Had Knight added "for driving chariots and showing off his pecs," she would have been more on the mark.

Ben-Hur became the all-time Oscar® champion, winning 11 of its 12 nominations. The achievement is worthy of note because we will never see its like again. Simply, pre–1967, there were more Oscars® to go around, what with Cinematography, Art Direction and Costume Design each carrying two awards—one each for color and black and white. Quite often the winners in the '40s and '50s would sweep through these categories because it was possible to honor the year's big movie without slighting other films. The biggest win possible in modern times seems to be the nine awards for *The Last Emperor*, which did it without a single acting award—or nomination. Several films have won eight—*Cabaret* (without the benefit of Best Picture), *Gandhi* and *Amadeus*.

When I interviewed Heston in the early '80s, he said that it would have been better if William Wyler had swapped pictures with Anthony Mann and directed *El Cid*, with Mann taking over *Ben-Hur*. Not because *Ben-Hur* would have been better, but, he felt, with Wyler directing *El Cid*, it might have been the best action movie of all time. This is very strange, because on the one hand, Mann, who directed a series of great Jimmy Stewart Westerns *(Winchester 73, Bend of the River)*, was probably the best action director of his era. On the other, Heston seems to be implying that *Ben-Hur*, which won Wyler a directing Oscar®, was virtually director proof.

Head Count: Edith slipping—two nominations, sixteen and seventeen, for *Career* and *The Five Pennies*, but no statuettes.

1960

Picture	The Alamo
	* The Apartment
	Elmer Gantry
	Sons and Lovers
	The Sundowners

Director	Jack Cardiff, Sons and Lovers
	Jules Dassin, Never on Sunday
	Alfred Hitchcock, Psycho
	* Billy Wilder, The Apartment
	Fred Zinneman, The Sundowners

Actor	Trevor Howard, Sons and Lovers
	* Burt Lancaster, Elmer Gantry
	Jack Lemmon, The Apartment
	Laurence Olivier, The Entertainer
	Spencer Tracy, Inherit the Wind

Actress	Greer Garson, Sunrise at Campobello
	Deborah Kerr, The Sundowners
	Shirley MacLaine, The Apartment
	Melina Mercouri, Never On Sunday
	* Elizabeth Taylor, Butterfield 8

Supporting Actor	Peter Falk, Murder, Inc.
	Jack Kruschen, The Apartment
	Sal Mineo, Exodus
	* Peter Ustinov, Spartacus
	Chill Wills, The Alamo

Supporting Actress	Glynis Johns, The Sundowners
	* Shirley Jones, Elmer Gantry
	Shirley Knight, The Dark at the Top of the Stairs
	Janet Leigh, Psycho
	Mary Ure, Sons and Lovers

Original Screenplay: Billy Wilder and I.A.L. Diamond, The Apartment

Adapted Screenplay: Richard Brooks, Elmer Gantry

Foreign Film: The Virgin Spring, Sweden, Ingmar Bergman

Cinematography: (black and white) Freddie Francis, Sons and Lovers
(color) Russell Metty, Spartacus

Left: Elizabeth Taylor, Best Actress, *Butterfield 8. Right:* Charles Laughton, Best Supporting Actor Peter Ustinov, and Jean Simmons in *Spartacus.*

Editing: Daniel Mandell, *The Apartment*

Score: (dramatic or comedy picture) Ernest Gold, *Exodus*
   (musical) Morris Stoloff and Harry Sukman, *Song Without End*

Original Song: "Never on Sunday," *Never on Sunday,* Manos Hadjidakis

Art Direction: (black and white) Alexander Trauner, *The Apartment*
   (color) Alexander Golitzen and Eric Orborn, *Spartacus*

Costume Design: (black and white) Edith Head and Edward Stevenson, *The Facts of Life*
   (color) Valles and Bill Thomas, *Spartacus*

Sound: *The Alamo,* Goldwyn Sound Dept., Todd–AO Sound Dept.

Short subjects: (cartoon) "Munro" (Jules Feiffer)
   (live action) "Days of the Painter"

Documentary: (feature) *The Horse with the Flying Tail*
   (short) Giuseppina

Special Effects: Gene Warren and Tim Baar, *The Time Machine*

Thalberg Award: Not given

Jean Hersholt Humanitarian Award: Sol Lesser

Honorary Oscar®: Gary Cooper.
Stan Laurel.
Hayley Mills, outstanding juvenile performance.

A legendary Oscar® year—Elizabeth Taylor had gone from America's sweetheart to the grieving widow of Mike Todd to that homewrecking tramp after she stole Eddie Fisher from Debbie Reynolds. Then she didn't want to play Gloria in *Butterfield 8,* which she thought salacious trash, both before and after it was made—she described the script as pornographic before she made it and said "it stinks" afterwards.

Then Liz got desperately ill, spent a month in a London hospital, and at one point endured a tracheotomy. Who else could possibly win Best Actress? Liz showed up for the Oscars® in a dress that showed off her tracheotomy scar and went home with the statuette. She was so heavily favored that Melina Mercouri decided to stay in Paris, Deborah Kerr stayed in Switzerland, and Shirley MacLaine felt there was no point in flying in from Japan to lose the race—though she did ask Taylor to accept for her, should she win.

Mercouri made one of the most ironic comments at the time, though no one would realize the irony until some years later. She had no desire to campaign for an Oscar®, saying "I'm an actress, not a politician." After the collapse of the junta and the return of democracy to Greece, Mercouri would become a member of Parliament and the Greek Minister of Culture.

For those readers under the age of 35, who have heard the title *Butterfield 8* and wondered what the hell it meant, back in the pre–digital age phone exchanges were named, not numbered— *Butterfield 8* (BU8 or 288) was the exchange that served the ritzier precincts of the Upper East Side of Manhattan.

Billy Wilder's *The Apartment,* however, was set on the Upper West Side of Manhattan, in the '60s of Central Park West, so nobody paid any attention to Wilder's unprecedented three Oscars®, as writer, producer and director of *The Apartment.*

Head Count: Head gets her touch back, wins seventh Oscar® for *The Facts of Life* (eighteenth nomination), must face bitter disappointment over nineteenth nomination, for *Pepe,* which fails to win.

|1961|

Picture	*Fanny*
	The Guns of Navarone
	The Hustler
	Judgment at Nuremberg
	*West Side Story

Picture
Fanny
The Guns of Navarone
The Hustler
Judgment at Nuremberg
* *West Side Story*

Director
Federico Fellini, *La Dolce Vita*
Stanley Kramer, *Judgment at Nuremberg*
Robert Rossen, *The Hustler*
J. Lee Thompson, *The Guns of Navarone*
* Robert Wise and Jerome Robbins, *West Side Story*

Actor
Charles Boyer, *Fanny*
Paul Newman, *The Hustler*
* Maximilian Schell, *Judgment at Nuremberg*
Spencer Tracy, *Judgment at Nuremberg*
Stuart Whitman, *The Mark*

Actress
Audrey Hepburn, *Breakfast at Tiffany's*
Piper Laurie, *The Hustler*
* Sophia Loren, *Two Women*
Geraldine Page, *Summer and Smoke*
Natalie Wood, *Splendor in the Grass*

Supporting Actor
* George Chakiris, *West Side Story*
Montgomery Clift, *Judgment at Nuremberg*
Peter Falk, *Pocketful of Miracles*
Jackie Gleason, *The Hustler*
George C. Scott, *The Hustler*

Supporting Actress
Fay Bainter, *The Children's Hour*
Judy Garland, *Judgment at Nuremberg*
Lotte Lenya, *The Roman Spring of Mrs. Stone*
Una Merkel, *Summer and Smoke*
* Rita Moreno, *West Side Story*

Original Screenplay: William Inge, *Splendor in the Grass*

Adapted Screenplay: Abby Mann, *Judgment at Nuremberg*

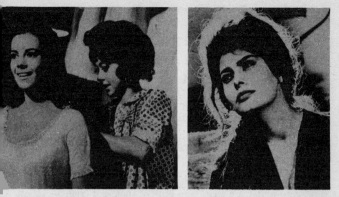

Left: Natalie Wood and Rita Moreno in Best Picture, *West Side Story. Right:* Sophia Loren, Best Actress for *Two Women.*

Foreign Film: *Through a Glass, Darkly*, Sweden, Ingmar Bergman

Cinematography: (black and white) Eugen Shuftan, *The Hustler*
(color) Daniel P. Fapp, *West Side Story*

Editing: Thomas Stanford, *West Side Story*

Score: (dramatic or comedy picture) Henry Mancini, *Breakfast at Tiffany's*
(musical) Saul Chaplin, Johnny Green, Sid Ramin and Irwin Kostal, *West Side Story*

Original Song: "Moon River," *Breakfast at Tiffany's*, Henry Mancini (music), Johnny Mercer (lyrics)

Art Direction: (black and white) Harry Horner, *The Hustler*
(color) Boris Leven, *West Side Story*

Costume Design: (black and white) Piero Gherardi, *La Dolce Vita*
(color) Irene Sharaff, *West Side Story*

Sound: *West Side Story*

Short subjects: (cartoon) "Ersatz" (Hungary)
(live action) "Seawards the Great Ships"

Documentary: (feature) *Sky Above and Mud Below*
(short) "Project Hope"

Special Effects: Bill Warrington (visual), Vivian C. Greenham (audio), *The Guns of Navarone*

Thalberg Award: Stanley Kramer

Jean Hersholt Humanitarian Award: George Seaton

Honorary Oscar®: William Hendricks for producing *A Force in Readiness*, a documentary on the Marine Corps.
Fred Metzler for outstanding service to the Academy.
Jerome Robbins for his choreography.

West Side Story becomes the last double-digit Oscar® winner, and becomes the only film with two directors ever to win best director. While there have been several occasions where people who have never met shared Oscars® in the writing categories—where writer B rewrote writer A's script and both of them got credit—Robert Wise and Jerome Robbins shared the directing Oscar® after Wise fired Robbins, whom he felt took far too long dealing with the dancers after Wise had the cameras ready to roll. When the two directors came to the podium, each was conspicuous in his absence from the other's thank you speech.

Sophia Loren became the only person to win an acting award for a film not in English, the Italian *Two Women*. In those days, the Oscars® were not broadcast in Europe—there were no broadcast satellites capable of beaming television programming around the world simultaneously—and Loren waited through the night to find out if she'd won. She got her notification, but not from the Academy. Cary Grant phoned her early the next morning to tell her she had won.

Signs of Trouble to Come: George C. Scott fulminated against the Oscars®, demanding that his name be withdrawn from competition. It was not, but he didn't win anyway.

Head Count: *Pocketful of Miracles* gives Edith Head an even score of nominations.

1962

Picture	*Lawrence of Arabia* *The Longest Day* *The Music Man* *Mutiny on the Bounty* *To Kill a Mockingbird*
Director	Pietro Germi, *Divorce—Italian Style* *David Lean, *Lawrence of Arabia* Robert Mulligan, *To Kill a Mockingbird* Arthur Penn, *The Miracle Worker* Frank Perry, *David and Lisa*
Actor	Burt Lancaster, *Bird Man of Alcatraz* Jack Lemmon, *Days of Wine and Roses* Marcello Mastroianni, *Divorce—Italian Style* Peter O'Toole, *Lawrence of Arabia* *Gregory Peck, *To Kill a Mockingbird*
Actress	*Anne Bancroft, *The Miracle Worker* Bette Davis, *Whatever Happened to Baby Jane?* Katharine Hepburn, *Long Day's Journey Into Night* Geraldine Page, *Sweet Bird of Youth* Lee Remick, *Days of Wine and Roses*
Supporting Actor	*Ed Begley, *Sweet Bird of Youth* Victor Buono, *What Ever Happened to Baby Jane?* Telly Savalas, *The Bird Man of Alcatraz* Omar Sharif, *Lawrence of Arabia* Terence Stamp, *Billy Budd*
Supporting Actress	Mary Badham, *To Kill a Mockingbird* *Patty Duke, *The Miracle Worker* Shirley Knight, *Sweet Bird of Youth* Angela Lansbury, *The Manchurian Candidate* Thelma Ritter, *Bird Man of Alcatraz*

Original Screenplay: Ennio de Concini, Alfredo Gianetti, Pietro Germi, *Divorce—Italian Style*

Left: Peter O'Toole in *Lawrence of Arabia*, Best Picture. *Right:* Oscar® winners Patty Duke and Anne Bancroft in *The Miracle Worker*.

Adapted Screenplay: Horton Foote, *To Kill a Mockingbird*

Foreign Film: *Sundays and Cybele*, France, Serge Bourguignon

Cinematography: (black and white) Jean Bourgoin and Walter Wottitz, *The Longest Day*
(color) Fred A. Young, *Lawrence of Arabia*

Editing: Anne Coates, *Lawrence of Arabia*

Score: (substantially original) Maurice Jarre, *Lawrence of Arabia*
(adaptation or treatment) Ray Heindorf, *The Music Man*

Original Song: "Days of Wine and Roses," *Days of Wine and Roses*, Henry Mancini (music), Johnny Mercer (lyrics)

Art Direction: (black and white) Alexander Golitzen and Henry Bumstead, *To Kill a Mockingbird*
(color) John Cox, *Lawrence of Arabia*

Costume Design: (black and white) Norma Koch, *What Ever Happened to Baby Jane?*
(color) Mary Wills, *The Wonderful World of the Brothers Grimm*

Sound: John Cox, Shepperton Sound Department, *Lawrence of Arabia*

Short subjects: (cartoon) "The Hole"
(live action) "Happy Anniversary"

Documentary: (feature) *Black Fox*
(short) "Dylan Thomas"

Special Effects: *The Longest Day*, Robert MacDonald (visual),
Jacques Maumont (audio)

Thalberg Award: Not given

Jean Hersholt Humanitarian Award: Not given

Rule Changes: Music Awards became designated as Score—Substantially Original and Scoring—Adaptation or Treatment.

The nominations in 1962 reveal how thoroughly tattered the studio system has become. Three of the big studio productions—*The Music Man, The Longest Day* and *Mutiny on the Bounty*—managed the uncommon achievement of being nominated as Best Picture without getting a single nomination in the writing, directing and acting categories. Only *Lawrence of Arabia* and *To Kill a Mockingbird* managed both direction and picture nominations, and the size and visual grandeur of *Lawrence* had a definite edge over the liberal restraint of *Mockingbird*.

Producer Sam Spiegel has an astonishing record in this decade—*The African Queen, On the Waterfront, The Bridge on the River Kwai, Suddenly, Last Summer* and *Lawrence of Arabia*. His films literally won more Oscars® than he made films. A producer who fled both his creditors and the Nazis and wandered into the U.S., Spiegel was widely regarded as a vulgarian—but when he met up with strong directors with strong projects, he was generally smart enough to stay out of their way. Of course, he doubtless preferred to spend time on his yacht in the Mediterranean than wander around the desert wondering about the water bill for the camels.

A note on actresses and age: When Robert Aldrich was shopping *Whatever Happened to Baby Jane?* to the studios, the general feeling was who wants to see washed up old stars like Bette Davis and Joan Crawford—they were, at the time, 54 and 56, respectively. That is, the same age as Jane Fonda in 1992, and not much older than Goldie Hawn, who's still swanning around playing semi-bimbos in tight jeans at 48. Angela Lansbury, who got a much deserved nomination for *The Manchurian Candidate*, was 37 when it was filmed. The actor playing her son, Lawrence Harvey, was 34.

Head Count: Twenty-two and counting—*The Man Who Shot Liberty Valence* and *My Geisha*, possibly the oddest imaginable double bill of 1962.

Picture	*America, America*
	Cleopatra
	How the West Was Won
	Lilies of the Field
	* *Tom Jones*
Director	Federico Fellini, *8½*
	Elia Kazan, *America America*
	Otto Preminger, *The Cardinal*
	* Tony Richardson, *Tom Jones*
	Martin Ritt, *Hud*
Actor	Albert Finney, *Tom Jones*
	Richard Harris, *This Sporting Life*
	Rex Harrison, *Cleopatra*
	Paul Newman, *Hud*
	* Sidney Poitier, *Lilies of the Field*
Actress	Leslie Caron, *The L–Shaped Room*
	Shirley MacLaine, *Irma La Douce*
	* Patricia Neal, *Hud*
	Rachel Roberts, *This Sporting Life*
	Natalie Wood, *Love with the Proper Stranger*
Supporting Actor	Nick Adams, *Twilight of Honor*
	Bobby Darin, *Captain Newman, M.D.*
	* Melvyn Douglas, *Hud*
	Hugh Griffith, *Tom Jones*
	John Huston, *The Cardinal*
Supporting Actress	Diane Cilento, *Tom Jones*
	Dame Edith Evans, *Tom Jones*
	Joyce Redman, *Tom Jones*
	* Margaret Rutherford, *The V.I.P.'s*
	Lilia Skala, *Lilies of the Field*

Original Screenplay: James R. Webb, *How the West Was Won*

Adapted Screenplay: John Osborne, *Tom Jones*

Foreign Film: *Federico Fellini's 8½*, Italy, Federico Fellini

Cinematography: (black and white) James Wong Howe, *Hud* (color) Leon Shamroy, *Cleopatra*

Editing: Harold F. Kress, *How the West Was Won*

Left: Sidney Poitier won Best Actor for *Lilies of the Field*. *Right:* Marcello Mastroianni in *8½*, Best Foreign Film.

Score: (original) John Addison, *Tom Jones*
(adaptation or treatment) Andre Previn, *Irma La Douce*

Original Song: "Call Me Irresponsible," *Papa's Delicate Condition*, James Van Heusen (music), Sammy Cahn (lyrics)

Art Direction: (black and white) Gene Callahan, *America, America*
(color) John De Cuir, Jack Martin Smith, Hilyard Brown, Herman Blumenthal, Steven Webb, Maurice Pelling and Boris Juraga, *Cleopatra*

Costume Design: (black and white) Piero Gherardi, *8½*
(color) Irene Sharaff, Vittorio Nino Novarese, Renie, *Cleopatra*

Sound: Franklin E. Milton, *How the West Was Won*

Short subjects: (cartoon) "The Critic"
(live action) "An Occurrence at Owl Creek Bridge"

Documentary: (feature) *Robert Frost, A Lover's Quarrel with the World*
(short) "Chagall"

Special Effects: Emil Kosa, *Cleopatra*

Thalberg Award: Sam Spiegel

Jean Hersholt Humanitarian Award: Not given

Rule Changes: The Special Effects category was split into Visual Effects and Sound Effects.

"It has been a long journey to this moment," said an awed Sidney Poitier, the first—and still the only—African-American to win for Best Actor. He deserved it four years later for *In the Heat of the Night*, his finest performance, but he wasn't even nominated. This was a momentous occasion in the best sense of the word. It seems strange that no one got excited over cinematographer James Wong Howe, who remains the only Chinese-American to win an Academy Award®—*Hud* was his second, the first had come in 1955 for *The Rose Tattoo*.

Hollywood went into shock this year, when *Tom Jones* led all nominees with ten nominations. While the community and the columnists had gone into hissy fits before about foreign (i.e. British) invasions before, no truly foreign film—as opposed to say, *Bridge on the River Kwai*, which had a big American star and Columbia money—had ever dominated the nominations before.

SEND 'EM BACK WHERE THEY CAME FROM!: Hollywood loves to give Oscars® to foreigners—at least, to foreign-born actors. Until the late '60s, when the Oscars® became dominated by American actors, it was a rare year that didn't see a few foreign born actors picking up prizes, going all the way back to Emil Jannings in '27–'28.

The following Oscar® winning actors were born outside the United States:

Peter Finch, Geoffrey Rush—Australia
Paul Muni, Luise Rainer (who both won in 1936!),
    Maxmilian Schell—Austria
Audrey Hepburn—Belgium
Charles Laughton, Victor McLaglen, Robert Donat,
    Ronald Colman, Donald Crisp, Edmund Gwenn, Laurence
    Olivier, Peter Ustinov, Alec Guinness, David Niven,
    Wendy Hiller, Richard Burton, Peter O'Toole, Hugh
    Griffith, Margaret Rutherford, Julie Andrews, Julie
    Christie, Paul Scofield, Maggie Smith, Glenda Jackson,
    John Mills, Vanessa Redgrave, John Gielgud, Ben
    Kingsley, Peggy Ashcroft, Michael Caine, Sean Connery,
    Jeremy Irons, Daniel Day-Lewis, Anthony Hopkins,
    Emma Thompson—Great Britain
Mary Pickford, Marie Dressler, Walter Huston, Anna
    Paquin—Canada
Dr. Haing S. Ngor—Cambodia
Claudette Colbert, Simone Signoret, Juliette Binoche—France

Katina Paxinou, Lila Kedrova—Greece
Paul Lukas—Hungary
Greer Garson, Barry Fitzgerald, Brenda Fricker—Ireland
Vivien Leigh—India
Anna Magnani, Sophia Loren—Italy
Olivia de Havilland, Joan Fontaine, Miyoshi
    Umecki—Japan
George Sanders, Yul Brynner—Russia
Ingrid Bergman—Sweden

There were two nominees for special effects, *Cleopatra*, which had a few nice dissolves, and *The Birds*, which was one of the great effects movies of its time. *Cleopatra* won the Oscar®.

Head Count: *Wives and Lovers, Love With the Proper Stranger, A New Kind of Love* make it 25 nominations for Edith Head.

1964

Picture	*Becket*
	Dr. Strangelove or: How I Learned to Stop Worrying and Love the Bomb
	Mary Poppins
	* *My Fair Lady*
	Zorba the Greek

Director	Michael Cacoyannis, *Zorba the Greek*
	* George Cukor, *My Fair Lady*
	Peter Glenville, *Becket*
	Stanley Kubrick, *Dr. Strangelove*
	Robert Stevenson, *Mary Poppins*

Actor	Richard Burton, *Becket*
	* Rex Harrison, *My Fair Lady*
	Peter O'Toole, *Becket*
	Anthony Quinn, *Zorba the Greek*
	Peter Sellers, *Dr. Strangelove*

Actress	*Julie Andrews, *Mary Poppins*
	Anne Bancroft, *The Pumpkin Eater*
	Sophia Loren, *Marriage—Italian Style*
	Debbie Reynolds, *The Unsinkable Molly Brown*
	Kim Stanley, *Seance on a Wet Afternoon*

Supporting Actor	John Gielgud, *Becket*
	Stanley Holloway, *My Fair Lady*
	Edmond O'Brien, *Seven Days in May*
	Lee Tracy, *The Best Man*
	*Peter Ustinov, *Topkapi*

Supporting Actress	Gladys Cooper, *My Fair Lady*
	Dame Edith Evans, *The Chalk Garden*
	Grayson Hall, *The Night of the Iguana*
	*Lila Kedrova, *Zorba the Greek*
	Agnes Moorehead, *Hush . . . Hush, Sweet Charlotte*

Original Screenplay: Peter Stone, Frank Tarloff, *Father Goose*

Adapted Screenplay: Edward Anhalt, *Becket*

Foreign Film: *Yesterday, Today and Tomorrow*, Italy, Vittorio de Sica

Left: Best Actor Rex Harrison, with co-star Audrey Hepburn, in *My Fair Lady. Right:* Best Picture, *My Fair Lady.* (Credit: *Movie Star News*)

Cinematography: (black and white) Walter Lassally, *Zorba the Greek*
(color), Harry Stradling, *My Fair Lady*

Editing: Cotton Warburton, *Mary Poppins*

Score: (original) Richard M. Sherman and Robert B. Sherman, *Mary Poppins*
(adaptation or treatment) Andre Previn, *My Fair Lady*

Original Song: Richard M. Sherman and Robert B. Sherman, "Chim Chim Cheree," *Mary Poppins*

Art Direction: (black and white) Vassilis Fotopoulos, *Zorba the Greek*
(color) Gene Allen and Cecil Beaton, *My Fair Lady*

Costume Design: (black and white) Dorothy Jeakins, *The Night of the Iguana*
(color) Cecil Beaton, *My Fair Lady*

Sound: George R. Groves, Warner Brothers Sound Dept., *My Fair Lady*

Sound Effects: Norman Wanastall, *Goldfinger*

Visual Effects: Peter Ellenshaw, Hamilton Luske and Eustace Lycett, *Mary Poppins*

Short subjects: (cartoon) "The Pink Phink" (The Pink Panther)
(live action) "Casals Conducts: 1964"

Documentary: (feature) *Jacques Cousteau's World Without Sun*
(short) "Nine from Little Rock"

Thalberg Award: Not given

Jean Hersholt Humanitarian Award: Not given

Honorary Oscar®: William Tuttle, for the makeup in *The 7 Faces of Dr. Lao*.

Non-singers who take singing roles in musicals can take a lesson from Natalie Wood and Audrey Hepburn. If you want to be honored, stroked and Oscar®ed, it is necessary to do one's own singing. Wood and Hepburn were two of the most admired stars in Hollywood, each starred in a huge, Oscar®-winning hit, and neither won the Oscar®. In fact, neither was even nominated, because they didn't do their own singing—their songs were performed by the great Marni Nixon, who should at some point have received an honorary Oscar® for her work on *West Side Story*, *My Fair Lady* and *Gentlemen Prefer Blondes*.

For the first time ever, all four acting categories were won by non-American actors, three Brits and Lila Kedrova, leading to Bob Hope's closing comment that "Hollywood has become a celluloid United Nations. The losers will now join hands and march on the British Embassy."

My Fair Lady was Warner Brothers' first Best Picture winner in 22 years—the last one had been *Casablanca*.

Head Count: Edith slipping badly—only two nominations this year, for *A House is Not a Home* and *What a Way to Go*. That made 27, but who's counting?

1965

Picture	*Darling*
	Doctor Zhivago
	Ship of Fools
	* *The Sound of Music*
	A Thousand Clowns

Director	David Lean, *Doctor Zhivago*
	John Schlesinger, *Darling*
	Hiroshi Teshigahara, *Woman in the Dunes*
	* Robert Wise, *The Sound of Music*
	William Wyler, *The Collector*

Actor	Richard Burton, *The Spy Who Came In From the Cold*
	* Lee Marvin, *Cat Ballou*
	Laurence Olivier, *Othello*
	Rod Steiger, *The Pawnbroker*
	Oskar Werner, *Ship of Fools*

Actress	Julie Andrews, *The Sound of Music*
	* Julie Christie, *Darling*
	Samantha Eggar, *The Collector*
	Elizabeth Hartman, *A Patch of Blue*
	Simone Signoret, *Ship of Fools*

Supporting Actor	*Martin Balsam, *A Thousand Clowns*
	Ian Bannen, *The Flight of the Phoenix*
	Tom Courtenay, *Doctor Zhivago*
	Michael Dunn, *Ship of Fools*
	Frank Finlay, *Othello*

Supporting Actress	Ruth Gordon, *Inside Daisy Clover*
	Joyce Redman, *Othello*
	Maggie Smith, *Othello*
	*Shelley Winters, *A Patch of Blue*
	Peggy Wood, *The Sound of Music*

Original Screenplay: Frederic Raphael, *Darling*

Adapted Screenplay: Robert Bolt, *Doctor Zhivago*

Foreign Film: *The Shop on Main Street*, Czechoslovakia, Jan Kadar

Left: Julie Andrews and Christopher Plummer in Best Picture, *The Sound of Music. Right:* Best Supporting Actor Lee Marvin in *Cat Ballou.*

Cinematography: (black and white) Ernest Laszlo, *Ship of Fools*
   (color) Freddie Young, *Doctor Zhivago*

Editing: William Reynolds, *The Sound of Music*

Score: (original) Maurice Jarre, *Doctor Zhivago*
   (adaptation or treatment) Irwin Kostal, *The Sound of Music*

Original Song: "The Shadow of Your Smile," *The Sandpiper,* Johnny Mandel (music), Paul Francis Webster (lyrics)

Art Direction: Robert Clatworthy, *Ship of Fools*
   (color) John Box and Terry Marsh, *Doctor Zhivago*

Costume Design: (black and white) Julie Harris, *Darling*
   (color) Phyllis Dalton, *Doctor Zhivago*

Sound: James P. Corcoran, Fred Hynes, *The Sound of Music*

Sound Effects: Tregoweth Brown, *The Great Race*

Visual Effects: John Stears, *Thunderball*

Short subjects: (cartoon) "The Dot and the Line"
   (live action) "The Chicken"

Documentary: (feature) *The Eleanor Roosevelt Story*
   (short) "To Be Alive!"

Thalberg Award: William Wyler

Jean Hersholt Humanitarian Award: Edmond L. DePatie

Honorary Oscar®: Bob Hope, for unique and distinguished
    service to the industry and the Academy.

The nominated films from the mid–'60s to the early '70s reveal
the increasingly schizophrenic nature of the film industry. Which
is the better picture, *Doctor Strangelove* or *Mary Poppins?* A low-
budget New York independent like *A Thousand Clowns* or *The
Sound of Music?* The way the Oscars® work, people must choose
between apples and oranges, which is why the Academy Awards®
drive the handicappers mad.

Consider the best actress category for 1965, the battle of the
Julies—did Julie Andrews, last year's winner for *Mary Poppins,*
top herself in *The Sound of Music,* or do we want to honor this
new, hipper, Julie Christie, all mod mini–skirts and alienation. To
understand the times, we would do well to remember that until
the Spielberg/Lucas monster hits of the '70s and '80s, *The Sound
of Music* was locked in battle with *Gone With the Wind* for the title
of top grossing movie of all time.

In this year of the first color telecast, Liza Minnelli made her
Academy Awards® debut, singing "What's New Pussycat."

Head Count: *Inside Daisy Clover* and *The Slender Thread* make it
29 nominations for Edith Head.

1966

Picture	*Alfie*
	* *A Man For All Seasons*
	The Russians Are Coming, The Russians Are Coming
	The Sand Pebbles
	Who's Afraid of Virginia Woolf?
Director	Michelangelo Antonioni, *Blow–Up*
	Richard Brooks, *The Professionals*
	Claude Lelouch, *A Man and a Woman*
	Mike Nichols, *Who's Afraid of Virginia Woolf?*
	* Fred Zinneman, *A Man for All Seasons*
Actor	Alan Arkin, *The Russians Are Coming, The Russians Are Coming*
	Richard Burton, *Who's Afraid of Virginia Woolf?*
	Michael Caine, *Alfie*
	Steve McQueen, *The Sand Pebbles*
	* Paul Scofield, *A Man for All Seasons*
Actress	Anouk Aimee, *A Man and a Woman*
	Ida Kaminska, *The Shop on Main Street*
	Lynn Redgrave, *Georgy Girl*
	Vanessa Redgrave, *Morgan!*
	* Elizabeth Taylor, *Who's Afraid of Virginia Woolf?*
Supporting Actor	Mako, *The Sand Pebbles*
	James Mason, *Georgy Girl*
	* Walter Matthau, *The Fortune Cookie*
	George Segal, *Who's Afraid of Virginia Woolf?*
	Robert Shaw, *A Man for All Seasons*
Supporting Actress	* Sandy Dennis, *Who's Afraid of Virginia Woolf?*
	Wendy Hiller, *A Man for All Seasons*
	Joclyn Lagarde, *Hawaii*
	Vivien Merchant, *Alfie*
	Geraldine Page, *You're a Big Boy Now*

Left: Best Actress Elizabeth Taylor with Richard Burton in *Who's Afraid of Virginia Wolf?*
Right: Orson Welles in Best Picture, *A Man for All Seasons.*

Original Screenplay: Claude Lelouch and Pierre Uytterhoeven, *A Man and a Woman*

Adapted Screenplay: Robert Bolt, *A Man for All Seasons*

Foreign Film: *A Man and a Woman*, France, Claude Lelouch

Cinematography: (black and white) Haskell Wexler, *Who's Afraid of Virginia Woolf?*
(color) Ted Moore, *A Man for All Seasons*

Editing: Fredric Steinkamp, Henry Berman, Stewart Linden, Frank Santillo, *Grand Prix*

Score: (original) John Barry, *Born Free*
(adaptation or treatment) Ken Thorne, *A Funny Thing Happened on the Way to the Forum*

Original Song: "Born Free," *Born Free*, John Barry (music), Don Black (lyrics)

Art Direction: (black and white) Richard Sylbert, *Who's Afraid of Virginia Woolf?*
(color) Jack Martin Smith and Dale Hennesy, *Fantastic Voyage*

Costume Design: (black and white) Irene Sharaff, *Who's Afraid of Virginia Woolf?*
(color) Elizabeth Jaffenden and Joan Bridge, *A Man for All Seasons*

185

Sound: Franklin P. Milton, *Grand Prix*

Visual Effects: Art Cruickshank, *Fantastic Voyage*

Sound Effects: Gordon Daniel, *Grand Prix*

Short subjects: (cartoon) "Herb Alpert and the Tijuana Brass
    Double Feature"
    (live action): "Wild Wings"

Documentary: (feature) *The War Game*
    (short) "A Year Toward Tomorrow"

Thalberg Award: Robert Wise

Jean Hersholt Humanitarian Award: George Bagnall

Honorary Oscar®: Y. Frank Freeman, for his service to the
    Academy.
    Yakima Canutt, for achievements as a stuntman.

In the Best Film category, the battle was between a big important
English theater adaptation and a big important American theat-
rical adaptation, with Hollywood veteran Fred Zinneman *(High
Noon, The Nun's Story)* pitted against brash newcomer Mike
Nichols. *Who's Afraid of Virginia Woolf?* was regarded as a daring taboo smasher in its day—Warner Brothers feared that the
film might be denied Production Code approval, and might gain
a condemned rating from the Catholic Church. Neither happened. Elizabeth Taylor won her second Oscar® by putting on 20
pounds and acting the shrew.

Though *Virginia Woolf* was regarded as daring, we might do
well to recall this contemporary comment from Andrew Sarris.
"Why Jack Warner should be applauded for bringing a Broadway
hit to the screen is a bit beyond me. I certainly won't hold my
breath until *The Zoo Story* and *The American Dream* materialize
on the screen as further manifestations of Jack Warner's addic-
tion to the Theater of the Absurd. From a Hollywood standpoint,
Virginia Woolf is no more daring a venture than *My Fair Lady*,
especially with Elizabeth Taylor and Richard Burton providing
box-office insurance."

Jack Valenti becomes the head of the Motion Pictures Producers Association of America (MPAA). Oscar®-cast watchers often
wonder who Jack Valenti is—why does he get to co–present the
Foreign Film Oscar® so often. Valenti is a Kennedy–era politico
who functions as the film industry's lobbyist and enforcer. When-
ever a foreign country (Canada, for instance, or France) starts
making noises about limiting local screen access for American
products, Valenti rides to the rescue.

This was the last year for the division of cinematography, art direction and costume design into color and black and white categories. *Who's Afraid of Virginia Woolf?* was the last black and white film to win Oscars® in these departments.

The '60s reach Hollywood: Black and white cinematography winner Haskell Wexler's acceptance speech includes the sentence "I hope we can use our art for peace and love."

The War Game, Peter Watkin's stunning vision of World War III, won an Academy Award® as Feature Documentary, and it isn't—it's a fiction film that uses documentary techniques, hand-held cameras, jittery edits, interviews, but the only way it's a documentary is if Britain was actually under nuclear attack in the mid-'60s.

Head Count: Edith wins her 30th nomination for *The Oscar*®, arguably the worst motion picture ever nominated for any award anywhere.

1967

Picture	*Bonnie and Clyde* *Doctor Dolittle* *The Graduate* *Guess Who's Coming to Dinner?* * *In the Heat of the Night*
Director	Richard Brooks, *In Cold Blood* Norman Jewison, *In the Heat of the Night* Stanley Kramer, *Guess Who's Coming to Dinner?* * Mike Nichols, *The Graduate* Arthur Penn, *Bonnie and Clyde*
Actor	Warren Beatty, *Bonnie and Clyde* Dustin Hoffman, *The Graduate* Paul Newman, *Cool Hand Luke* * Rod Steiger, *In the Heat of the Night* Spencer Tracy, *Guess Who's Coming to Dinner?*
Actress	Anne Bancroft, *The Graduate* Faye Dunaway, *Bonnie and Clyde* Dame Edith Evans, *The Whisperers* Audrey Hepburn, *Wait Until Dark* * Katherine Hepburn, *Guess Who's Coming to Dinner?*
Supporting Actor	John Cassavetes, *The Dirty Dozen* Gene Hackman, *Bonnie and Clyde* Cecil Kellaway, *Guess Who's Coming to Dinner* * George Kennedy, *Cool Hand Luke* Michael J. Pollard, *Bonnie and Clyde*
Supporting Actress	Carol Channing, *Thoroughly Modern Millie* Mildred Natwick, *Barefoot in the Park* * Estelle Parsons, *Bonnie and Clyde* Beah Richards, *Guess Who's Coming to Dinner?* Katharine Ross, *The Graduate*

Original Screenplay: William Rose, *Guess Who's Coming to Dinner?*

Left: Mike Nichols, Best Director, *The Graduate. Right:* Irving Thalberg Award winner Alfred Hitchcock.

Adapted Screenplay: Stirling Silliphant, *In the Heat of the Night*

Foreign Film: *Closely Watched Trains*, Czechoslovakia, Jiri Menzel

Cinematography: Burnett Guffey, *Bonnie and Clyde*

Editing: Hal Ashby, *In the Heat of the Night*

Score: (original) Elmer Bernstein, *Thoroughly Modern Millie* (adaptation or treatment) Alfred Newman and Ken Darby, *Camelot*

Original Song: "Talk to the Animals," *Doctor Dolittle*, Leslie Bricusse

Art Direction: John Truscott and Edward Carrere, *Camelot*

Costume Design: John Truscott, *Camelot*

Sound: Goldwyn Sound Department, *In the Heat of the Night*

Visual Effects: L.B. Abbott, *Doctor Dolittle*

Sound Effects: John Poyner, *The Dirty Dozen*

Short subjects: (cartoon) "The Box" (live action) "A Place To Stand"

Documentary: (feature) *The Anderson Platoon* (short) "The Redwoods"

Thalberg Award: Alfred Hitchcock

Jean Hersholt Humanitarian Award: Gregory Peck

Honorary Oscar®: Arthur Freed, for service to the Academy and the production of six awards telecasts.

Rule Changes: Categories were no longer divided between black and white and color films.

Tragedy delayed the Academy Awards® show for two days when Martin Luther King was assassinated. Numerous members of the film community wanted to go to the funeral, which was scheduled for one day after the Oscars®. The Academy delayed the broadcast until after the funeral.

The '60s hit Hollywood, 2: Editing winner Hal Ashby quoted Haskell Wexler's peace and love speech. Sammy Davis, Jr., performs Best Song nominee "If I Could Talk to the Animals" dressed in the Oscar® show's first Nehru jacket. Groovy. In his acceptance speech, Rod Steiger thanks the Maharishi. *The Anderson Platoon*, winner of best documentary feature, is the first film on Vietnam to win an Oscar®. It's French, and it's anti-war.

But to some people, it's still the '40s: Bob Hope's all-time best Oscar® show one-liner—"Welcome to the Academy Awards®, or as it's known at my house, Passover."

Head Count: For the first time since the inception of the category, Edith Head is not nominated for an Oscar®. 30 nominations in 19 years—and seven wins—stands as one of the most impressive achievements in Academy history. Not repeatable today, as two Costume Design Oscars® were given most years, but in the single award era, Head would pick up four more nominations *(Sweet Charity, The Sting, The Man Who Would Be King, Airport '77)* and win her eighth Oscar® for *The Sting*.

Picture	*Funny Girl*
	The Lion in Winter
	*Oliver!
	Rachel, Rachel
	Romeo and Juliet
Director	Anthony Harvey, *The Lion in Winter*
	Stanley Kubrick, *2001: A Space Odyssey*
	Gillo Pontecorvo, *The Battle of Algiers*
	*Carol Reed, *Oliver!*
	Franco Zeffirelli, *Romeo and Juliet*
Actor	Alan Arkin, *The Heart is a Lonely Hunter*
	Alan Bates, *The Fixer*
	Ron Moody, *Oliver!*
	Peter O'Toole, *The Lion in Winter*
	*Cliff Robertson, *Charly*
Actress	*Katharine Hepburn, *The Lion in Winter*
	Patricia Neal, *The Subject Was Roses*
	Vanessa Redgrave, *Isadora*
	*Barbra Streisand, *Funny Girl*
	Joanne Woodward, *Rachel, Rachel*
Supporting Actor	*Jack Albertson, *The Subject Was Roses*
	Seymour Cassel, *Faces*
	Daniel Massey, *Star!*
	Jack Wild, *Oliver!*
	Gene Wilder, *The Producers*
Supporting Actress	Lynn Carlin, *Faces*
	*Ruth Gordon, *Rosemary's Baby*
	Sondra Locke, *The Heart is a Lonely Hunter*
	Kay Medford, *Funny Girl*
	Estelle Parsons, *Rachel, Rachel*

Original Screenplay: Mel Brooks, *The Producers*

Adapted Screenplay: James Goldman, *The Lion in Winter*

Foreign Film: *War and Peace*, USSR, Sergei Bondarchuk

Above: Best Visual Effects winner, *2001: A Space Odyssey. Right:* Barbra Streisand won the award for Best Actress in *Funny Girl.*

Cinematography: Pasqualino De Santis, *Romeo and Juliet*

Editing: Frank P. Keller, *Bullitt*

Score: (original score, non-musical) John Barry, *The Lion in Winter*
(musical picture, original or adapted) John Green, *Oliver!*

Original Song: "The Windmills of Your Mind," *The Thomas Crown Affair,* Michel Legrand
(music) Alan and Marilyn Bergman, lyrics

Art Direction: John Box and Terence Marsh, *Oliver!*

Costume Design: Danilo Donati, *Romeo and Juliet*

Sound: Shepperton Studio Sound Department, *Oliver!*

Short subjects: (cartoons) "Winnie the Pooh and the Blustery Day"
(live action) "Robert Kennedy Remembered"

Documentary: (feature) *Journey Into Self*
(short) "Why Man Creates"

Visual Effects: Stanley Kubrick, *2001: A Space Odyssey*

Thalberg Award: Not given

Jean Hersholt Humanitarian Award: Martha Raye

Honorary Oscar®: John Chambers for the makeup in *Planet of the Apes*.
Onna White, for the choreography of *Oliver!*

There was a sizeable gasp when Ingrid Bergman opened the Best Actress envelope and announced the first major category tie in 37 years. Bergman herself was more than a little surprised, though the advice from the Price–Waterhouse representative—that she should be sure to "read everything" made more sense in hindsight than it had beforehand.

The numbers:
11—number of hosts at the 1968 Academy Awards®.
—number of Best Actress nominations for Katharine Hepburn, putting her ahead of Bette Davis as the most nominated performer.
36—number of years between Katharine Hepburn's first and second Oscars®.
453—In minutes, the length of Sergei Bondarchuk's mammoth Soviet adaptation of *War and Peace*, the longest Oscar®–winning film ever.

Odd Fates of Oscar® winners: Best supporting actor Jack Albertson spends the twilight of his career playing second banana to Freddie Prinze on the situation comedy "Chico and the Man."

Like Stonehenge and those flattened circles in fields in England, *Oliver!*'s astonishing victory for Best Picture and Director remains one of the inexplicable anomalies of life here on spaceship earth. Carol Reed never won for *The Third Man, The Man Between, The Fallen Idol, Outcast of the Islands,* any of his great films of the '40s and '50s, yet he won for *Oliver!*?

1969

Picture	*Anne of the Thousand Days* *Butch Cassidy and the Sundance Kid* *Hello, Dolly!* * *Midnight Cowboy* *Z*
Director	Costa–Gavras, *Z* George Roy Hill, *Butch Cassidy and the Sundance Kid* Arthur Penn, *Alice's Restaurant* Sydney Pollack, *They Shoot Horses, Don't They?* * John Schlesinger, *Midnight Cowboy*
Actor	Richard Burton, *Anne of the Thousand Days* Dustin Hoffman, *Midnight Cowboy* Peter O'Toole, *Goodbye, Mr. Chips* Jon Voight, *Midnight Cowboy* * John Wayne, *True Grit*
Actress	Genevieve Bujold, *Anne of the Thousand Days* Jane Fonda, *They Shoot Horses, Don't They?* Liza Minnelli, *The Sterile Cuckoo* Jean Simmons, *The Happy Ending* * Maggie Smith, *The Prime of Miss Jean Brodie*
Supporting Actor	Rupert Crosse, *The Reivers* Elliot Gould, *Bob & Carol & Ted & Alice* Jack Nicholson, *Easy Rider* Anthony Quayle, *Anne of the Thousand Days* * Gig Young, *They Shoot Horses, Don't They?*
Supporting Actress	Catharine Burns, *Last Summer* Dyan Cannon, *Bob & Carol & Ted & Alice* * Goldie Hawn, *Cactus Flower* Sylvia Miles, *Midnight Cowboy* Susannah York, *They Shoot Horses, Don't They?*

Left: John Wayne, Best Actor, *True Grit. Right:* Goldie Hawn won Best Supporting Actress for *Cactus Flower.*

Original Screenplay: William Goldman, *Butch Cassidy and the Sundance Kid*

Adapted Screenplay: Waldo Salt, *Midnight Cowboy*

Foreign Film: *Z*, Algeria, Costa–Gavras

Cinematography: Conrad Hall, *Butch Cassidy and the Sundance Kid*

Editing: Francoise Bonnot, *Z*

Score: (original, non-musical) Burt Bacharach, *Butch Cassidy and the Sundance Kid*
(original or adaptation) Lionel Newman and Lennie Hayton, *Hello, Dolly!*

Original Song: "Raindrops Keep Falling on My Head," *Butch Cassidy and the Sundance Kid*, Burt Bacharach, music, Hal David, lyrics

Art Direction: John DeCuir, Jack Martin Smith and Herman Blumenthal, *Hello, Dolly!*

Custume Design: Margaret Furse, *Anne of the Thousand Days*

Sound: Jack Solomon and Murray Spivack, *Hello, Dolly!*

Visual Effects: Robbie Robertson, *Marooned*

Short subjects: (cartoon) "It's Tough to be a Bird"
(live action) "The Magic Machines"

Documentary: (feature) *Arthur Rubinstein, The Love of Life*
(short) "Czechoslovakia, 1968"

Thalberg Award: Not given

Jean Hersholt Humanitarian Award: George Jessel

Honorary Oscar®: Cary Grant.

One of the biggest changes to hit Hollywood occurred when the MPAA changed from having a code of conduct for movies to a rating system. These days, when an X–rating means pornography, we often forget that originally the "X" simply meant for adults only, no one under the age of eighteen admitted. Had the MPAA copyrighted the "X," as they did with PG and G, there would never have been any problem, because porno producers, who entered the mainstream in 1972, could not have used the "X." But they didn't, so Hollywood became terrified of the "X" and of its successor, the NC-17.

We should remember this because in 1969, *Midnight Cowboy* became the only X–rated film ever to win Best Picture—*Midnight Cowboy* looks pretty tame in the age of *Basic Instinct*, but at the time it was pretty daring. Even today it would probably be a hard R.

1969 also provides a cool bit of synchronicity, for the winning year for *Midnight Cowboy* was also the last great year for the Hollywood Western. *Butch Cassidy and the Sundance Kid* won screenplay, score and song, John Wayne finally winning a best actor Oscar® for *True Grit* (which Wayne called "the easiest role of my career") and nominations for *The Wild Bunch*. Also, Wayne won his Oscar® the same year Jane "Hanoi Hannah" Fonda got her first best actress nomination.

Had there been an Academy Award® for most successful nomination campaign, or best buffet, Universal's mega–campaign for their flop period picture, *Anne of the Thousand Days*, would surely have won. In the year of *Easy Rider* and *Midnight Cowboy*, despite box office failure and a critical response that ranged from indifference to contempt, *Anne of the Thousand Days* grabbed the most nominations of any picture at the 1969 Academy Awards®. Universal's special screenings included a ritzy supper with each screening. If people in Hollywood know on which side their bread is buttered, they also know what to do when they are given free filet mignon.

1970

Picture	*Airport*
	Five Easy Pieces
	Love Story
	M*A*S*H
	* *Patton*

Director	Robert Altman, *M*A*S*H*
	Federico Fellini, *Fellini Satyricon*
	Arthur Hiller, *Love Story*
	Ken Russell, *Women in Love*
	* Franklin J. Schaffner, *Patton*

Actor	Melvyn Douglas, *I Never Sang for My Father*
	James Earl Jones, *The Great White Hope*
	Jack Nicholson, *Five Easy Pieces*
	Ryan O'Neal, *Love Story*
	* George C. Scott, *Patton*

Actress	Jane Alexander, *The Great White Hope*
	* Glenda Jackson, *Women in Love*
	Ali MacGraw, *Love Story*
	Sarah Miles, *Ryan's Daughter*
	Carrie Snodgress, *Diary of a Mad Housewife*

Supporting Actor	Richard Castellano, *Lovers and Other Strangers*
	Chief Dan George, *Little Big Man*
	Gene Hackman, *I Never Sang for My Father*
	John Marley, *Love Story*
	* John Mills, *Ryan's Daughter*

Supporting Actress	Karen Black, *Five Easy Pieces*
	Lee Grant, *The Landlord*
	* Helen Hayes, *Airport*
	Sally Kellerman, *M*A*S*H*
	Maureen Stapleton, *Airport*

Original Screenplay: Francis Ford Coppola and Edmund H. North, *Patton*

Adapted Screenplay: Ring Lardner, Jr., *M*A*S*H*

Left: Honorary Oscar® winner Orson Welles. *Right:* Best Actor George C. Scott in *Patton.*

Foreign Film: *Investigation of a Citizen Above Suspicion*, Italy, Elio Petri

Cinematography: Freddie Young, *Ryan's Daughter*

Editing: Hugh S. Fowler, *Patton*

Score: (original) Francis Lai, *Love Story*
(original song score) The Beatles, *Let It Be*

Original Song: "For All We Know," *Lovers and Other Strangers*, Fred Karlin (music), Rob Royer and James Griffin (lyrics)

Art Direction: Urie McCleary and Gil Parrondo, *Patton*

Costume Design: Nino Novarese, *Cromwell*

Sound: Douglas Williams and Don Bassman, *Patton*

Short subjects: (cartoon) "Is It Always Right to Be Right?"
(live action) "The Resurrection of Broncho Billy" (John Carpenter)

Documentary: (feature) *Woodstock*
(short) "Interviews with My Lai Veterans"

Visual Effects: A.D. Flowers and L.B. Abbott, *Tora! Tora! Tora!*

Thalberg Award: Ingmar Bergman

Jean Hersholt Humanitarian Award: Frank Sinatra

Honorary Oscar®: Lillian Gish.
Orson Welles.

"Oh my god," gasped Goldie Hawn. "It's George C. Scott!" According to the late Paul Rosenfield, a Hollywood gossip columnist and author of *The Club Rules*, the powers that be in Hollywood want what they can't have, and George C. Scott made it plain, time and again, that, in political terms, if nominated he would not run and if elected he would not serve. So they gave him the Oscar®.

1970 was a great year for big gaps between first and second Oscars®—Ring Lardner, Jr.'s win for *M*A*S*H* came 29 years after his win for *Woman of the Year*, and Helen Hayes' Supporting Actress turn in *Airport* came a mere 39 years after her victory in *The Sin of Madelon Claudet*.

One Oscar®-winning film leads to another. President Richard Nixon screened *Patton* a couple of times in the White House screening room and then he invaded Cambodia. This led to *New York Times* reporter Sidney Schanberg's trip to Cambodia to cover the war. When the Khmer Rouge took over, they sent Schanberg's translator, Dith Pran, to a re–education camp, from which he escaped. This led directly to Schanberg's article, "The Death and Life of Dith Pran," which led to a movie deal with David Puttnam, which led to the movie *The Killing Fields*, which led to many Oscars®. If it weren't for the Best Picture of 1970, we never would have heard of Dr. Haing S. Ngor. If one wishes to stretch the logic of this, if Nixon had not decided to invade Cambodia, the Khmer Rouge might never have won, and Dr. Ngor would still be a gynecologist in Phnom Penh. On top of that, if *The Killing Fields* had never been made, we would have been deprived of Spalding Grey's *Swimming To Cambodia*, and we might never have heard of Spalding Grey, either!

Orson Welles received a special Oscar® honoring his contributions to the art of motion pictures, but he said he couldn't show up—he was supposedly in Spain working on his never completed *The Other Side of the Wind*, so John Huston accepted the award for him and Welles thanked the Academy on film. The joke was on the Academy. Welles was in his house in Hollywood, and Huston gave him the award at dinner after the show.

1971

Picture	A Clockwork Orange Fiddler on the Roof * The French Connection The Last Picture Show Nicholas and Alexandra
Director	Peter Bogdanovich, The Last Picture Show * William Friedkin, The French Connection Norman Jewison, Fiddler on the Roof Stanley Kubrick, A Clockwork Orange John Schlesinger, Sunday, Bloody Sunday
Actor	Peter Finch, Sunday, Bloody Sunday * Gene Hackman, The French Connection Walter Matthau, Kotch George C. Scott, The Hospital Topol, Fiddler on the Roof
Actress	Julie Christie, McCabe and Mrs. Miller * Jane Fonda, Klute Glenda Jackson, Sunday, Bloody Sunday Vanessa Redgrave, Mary, Queen of Scots Janet Suzman, Nicholas and Alexandra
Supporting Actor	Jeff Bridges, The Last Picture Show Leonard Frey, Fiddler on the Roof Richard Jaeckel, Sometimes a Great Notion * Ben Johnson, The Last Picture Show Roy Scheider, The French Connection
Supporting Actress	Ellen Burstyn, The Last Picture Show Barbara Harris, Who is Harry Kellerman, and Why is He Saying Those Terrible Things About Me? * Cloris Leachman, The Last Picture Show Margaret Leighton, The Go-Between Ann-Margret, Carnal Knowledge

Left: William Friedkin, Best Director, *The French Connection*. *Right:* Best Actor Gene Hackman in *The French Connection*.

Original Screenplay: Paddy Chayefsky, *The Hospital*

Adapted Screenplay: Ernest Tidyman, *The French Connection*

Foreign Film: *The Garden of the Finzi–Continis*, Italy, Vittorio De Sica

Cinematography: Oswald Morris, *Fiddler on the Roof*

Editing: Jerry Greenberg, *The French Connection*

Score: (original dramatic score) Michel Legrand, *Summer of '42*
(adaptation and original song score) John Williams, *Fiddler on the Roof*

Original Song: "Theme from Shaft," Isaac Hayes, *Shaft*

Art Direction: John Box, Ernest Archer, Jack Maxsted and Gil Parrondo, *Nicholas and Alexandra*

Costume Design: Yvonne Blake and Anthony Castillo, *Nicholas and Alexandra*

Sound: Gordon K. McCallum and David Hildyard, *Fiddler on the Roof*

Short subjects: (animated) "The Crunch Bird"
(live action) "The Sentinels of Silence"

Documentary: (feature) *The Hellstrom Chronicle*
(short) "The Sentinels of Silence"

Visual Effects: Alan Maley, Eustace Lycett and Danny Lee,
   Bedknobs and Broomsticks

Thalberg Award: Not given

Jean Hersholt Humanitarian Award: Not given

Honorary Oscar®: Charles Chaplin.

The Academy honored a new generation of stars in 1971—Jane
Fonda, Gene Hackman and director William Friedkin. But they
didn't forget the old—Best Supporting Actor Ben Johnson had
starred in some Westerns in the late '40s and early '50s (John
Ford's *Wagonmaster*, most notably) and then disappeared from
view until his career was revived by Sam Peckinpah and then
Peter Bogdanovich, who cast him as Sam the Lion in *The Last
Picture Show*.

But a ghost from deep in Hollywood's past provided the most
emotionally electrifying moment in the living memory of Oscars®.
An octogenarian Charlie Chaplin returned to America for the first
time in three decades and received an Honorary Oscar® and a five
minute standing ovation as he stood on the stage at the Dorothy
Chandler Pavilion.

Isaac Hayes became the first African–American to win a music
Oscar®, for the "Theme from Shaft." William Friedkin became
the youngest best director winner at age 32. Jane Fonda, who
made a subdued and remarkably polite acceptance speech
("There's a great deal to say, but I'm not going to say it tonight.") had two factors in her favor, aside from her performance—she is Hollywood royalty, whatever people thought of her
politics, and she was the only American nominated for Best Actress.

Everyone talks about *Citizen Kane* losing best picture to *How
Green Was My Valley*. Here, however, is a far greater injustice.
The Hellstrom Chronicle beat *The Sorrow and the Pity*. *The Hellstrom Chronicle* is a bug documentary with an apocalyptic narra-
tion. It has fantastic cinematography, sure, but it's still just a
movie about bugs. *The Sorrow and the Pity*, which often turns up
on Greatest Films of All Times lists, is a morally challenging
investigation of the occupation of France during World War II.
(The Academy sort of made up to *Sorrow* director Marcel Ophuls
20 years later, when they honored him for *Hotel Terminus*.)

1972

Picture	*Cabaret*
	Deliverance
	The Emigrants
	* *The Godfather*
	Sounder
Director	John Boorman, *Deliverance*
	Francis Ford Coppola, *The Godfather*
	*Bob Fosse, *Cabaret*
	Joseph L. Mankiewicz, *Sleuth*
	Jan Troell, *The Emigrants*
Actor	*Marlon Brando, *The Godfather*
	Michael Caine, *Sleuth*
	Laurence Olivier, *Sleuth*
	Peter O'Toole, *The Ruling Class*
	Paul Winfield, *Sounder*
Actress	*Liza Minnelli, *Cabaret*
	Diana Ross, *Lady Sings the Blues*
	Maggie Smith, *Travels with My Aunt*
	Cicely Tyson, *Sounder*
	Liv Ullman, *The Emigrants*
Supporting Actor	Eddie Albert, *The Heartbreak Kid*
	James Caan, *The Godfather*
	Robert Duvall, *The Godfather*
	*Joel Grey, *Cabaret*
	Al Pacino, *The Godfather*
Supporting Actress	Jeannie Berlin, *The Heartbreak Kid*
	*Eileen Heckart, *Butterflies are Free*
	Geraldine Page, *Pete 'N' Tillie*
	Susan Tyrrell, *Fat City*
	Shelley Winters, *The Poseidon Adventure*

Original Screenplay: Jeremy Larner, *The Candidate*

Adapted Screenplay: Mario Puzo and Francis Ford Coppola, *The Godfather*

Foreign Film: *The Discreet Charm of the Bourgeoisie*, France, Luis Bunuel

Cinematography: Geoffrrey Unsworth, *Cabaret*

Editing: David Bretherton, *Cabaret*

Left: Best Actor Marlon Brando, *The Godfather. Right:* Liza Minnelli won the Best Actress Oscar® for *Cabaret.*

Score: (original dramatic score) Charles Chaplin, *Limelight*
    (adaptation or original song score) Ralph Burns, *Cabaret*

Original Song: "The Morning After," *The Poseidon Adventure,*
    Al Kasha and Joel Hirschhorn

Art Direction: Rolf Zehetbauer and Jurgen Kiebach, *Cabaret*

Costume Design: Anthony Powell, *Travels with My Aunt*

Sound: Robert Knudsen and David Hilyard, *Cabaret*

Short subjects: (animated) "A Christmas Carol"
    (live action) "Norman Rockwell's World"

Documentary: (feature) *Marjoe*
    (short) "This Tiny World"

Visual Effects: L.B. Abbott and A.D. Flowers, *The Poseidon
    Adventure*

Thalberg Award: Not given

Jean Hersholt Humanitarian Award: Rosalind Russell

Honorary Oscar®: Edward G. Robinson.
    Charles S. Boren, film industry labor negotiator.

Rule Changes: The category Special Visual Effects became a
"Special Achievement Award," not given every year.

You're going out there a movie star kid, but when you're done,
you'll look like a jerk. Charlton Heston was scheduled as the first

host of the Oscars® in 1972, but when he got trapped in traffic, Clint Eastwood substituted. Eastwood was not prepared—it wasn't his fault—and he was stuck with Charlton Heston's material, which made no sense at all. Eastwood decided that he would not return unless nominated. It took a while—twenty years, to be exact—before Eastwood came back in glory.

In a rare moment of valuing style over substance, the Academy voters disagreed with the Directors' Guild, which had honored Francis Ford Coppola for *The Godfather*. People think of 1972 as being the year of *The Godfather* because of its wins for picture, actor and adapted screenplay. But those were all its wins—*Cabaret* swamped it, with eight Oscars®, including director, actress, supporting actor, art direction, and cinematography. *Cabaret* stands in an unenviable position—the most Oscars® won by a film that did not win Best Picture. This also marks the start of another Oscar® pattern. Bob Fosse was nominated as Best Director three times, in 1972, 1974 and 1979, and every time he found himself in direct competition with Francis Coppola—'72 was his good year, when he won the Oscar®, Tony and Emmy.

Until Angela Bassett's 1993 nomination for *What's Love Got to Do With It?*, it was literally possible to count the number of black women nominated for best actress on the fingers of one hand— Dorothy Dandridge in *Carmen Jones*, Diahann Carroll in *Claudine*, Whoopi Goldberg in *The Color Purple*, and 1972's brace of nominees, Diana Ross and Cicely Tyson, a pairing that effectively wrecked both their chances of winning.

These awards were the Sacheen Littlefeather Oscars®. Brando designated Ms. Littlefeather to accept for him. He could not accept because of Hollywood and American society's treatment of Native Americans. Littlefeather was not, it turned out, an Indian activist, but a B–movie actress who would later appear in *Playboy* magazine.

1973

Picture	*American Graffiti*
	Cries and Whispers
	The Exorcist
	* *The Sting*
	A Touch of Class
Director	Ingmar Bergman, *Cries and Whispers*
	Bernardo Bertolucci, *Last Tango in Paris*
	William Friedkin, *The Exorcist*
	* George Roy Hill, *The Sting*
	George Lucas, *American Graffiti*
Actor	Marlon Brando, *Last Tango in Paris*
	* Jack Lemmon, *Save the Tiger*
	Jack Nicholson, *The Last Detail*
	Al Pacino, *Serpico*
	Robert Redford, *The Sting*
Actress	Ellen Burstyn, *The Exorcist*
	* Glenda Jackson, *A Touch of Class*
	Marsha Mason, *Cinderella Liberty*
	Barbra Streisand, *The Way We Were*
	Joanne Woodward, *Summer Wishes, Winter Dreams*
Supporting Actor	Vincent Gardenia, *Bang the Drum Slowly*
	Jack Gilford, *Save the Tiger*
	* John Houseman, *The Paper Chase*
	Jason Miller, *The Exorcist*
	Randy Quaid, *The Last Detail*
Supporting Actress	Linda Blair, *The Exorcist*
	Candy Clark, *American Graffiti*
	Madeline Kahn, *Paper Moon*
	* Tatum O'Neal, *Paper Moon*
	Sylvia Sidney, *Summer Wishes, Winter Dreams*

Original Screenplay: David S. Ward, *The Sting*

Adapted Screenplay: William Peter Blatty, *The Exorcist*

Foreign Film: *Day For Night*, France, Francois Truffaut

Top: Paul Newman and Robert Redford in Best Picture, *The Sting. Bottom:* Best Actress Glenda Jackson with George Segal in *A Touch of Class.*

Cinematography: Sven Nykvist, *Cries and Whispers*

Editing: William Reynolds, *The Sting*

Score: (original dramatic score) Marvin Hamlisch, *The Way We Were*

(original song score or adaptation) Marvin Hamlisch, *The Sting*

Original Song: "The Way We Were," *The Way We Were,* Marvin Hamlisch, music, Alan and Marilyn Bergman, lyrics

Art Direction: Henry Bumstead, *The Sting*

Costume Design: Edith Head, *The Sting*

Sound: Robert Knudsen and Chris Newman, *The Exorcist*

Short subjects: (animated) "Frank Film"
(live action) "The Bolero"

Documentary: (feature) *The Great American Cowboy*
(short) "Princeton: A Search for Answers"

Thalberg Award: Lawrence Weingarten

Jean Hersholt Humanitarian Award: Lew Wasserman

Honorary Oscar®: Henri Langlois, founder of the
Cinematheque Francais.
Groucho Marx.

The answer is Robert Opal. The question is "Who streaked the
Academy Awards® in 1973?" Like "Sacheen Littlefeather" and
the "deaf" children who signed "You Light Up My Life" with
Debbie Boone who turned out to be neither deaf nor signing
anything that had anything to do with the song, remarks about
"Zionist hoodlums" and congratulatory telegrams from North
Vietnam, Opal belongs to the list of gross embarrassments that
plagued the Academy in the '70s. For the record, Opal streaked
between the Acting Awards, leading David Niven to remark that
"the only laugh that man will probably ever get is for stripping
and showing off his shortcomings."

There was a certain degree of confusion among the presenters,
which should come as no surprise when the winners of supporting
actor and actress were the youngest competitive winners ever and
one of the oldest newcomers Hollywood had ever seen.

Tatum O'Neal gave her Oscar®-winning performance at age
nine in Peter Bogdanovich's *Paper Moon*, though Bogdanovich
should have gotten a share of it—Bogdanovich is a remarkably
economical director, but there are scenes in *Paper Moon* that took
dozens of takes before O'Neal gave the performance he wanted.
O'Neal's Oscar® marks the most extreme case ever of a lead performance winning a supporting Academy Award®—she's in virtually every frame of the film. John Houseman, at age 70, was
plucked from the relative obscurity of Juilliard to play an intellec-
tually sadistic law professor in James Bridges' *The Paper Chase*.
Just think. If James Mason hadn't declined the part, and Edward
G. Robinson hadn't been dying, we might never had heard all
those commercials featuring Houseman's impeccable accent.

The Academy begins its decade-long infatuation with the one-
note performances of Marsha Mason, who picks up the first of her
four Best Actress nominations for *Cinderella Liberty*. For the first
time, Katharine Hepburn attends the ceremony to present producer Lawrence Weingarten with the Thalberg Award.

Picture	*Chinatown*
	The Conversation
	* *The Godfather, Part II*
	Lenny
	The Towering Inferno
Director	John Cassavetes, *A Woman Under the Influence*
	* Francis Ford Coppola, *The Godfather, Part II*
	Bob Fosse, *Lenny*
	Roman Polanski, *Chinatown*
	Francois Truffaut, *Day For Night*
Actor	* Art Carney, *Harry and Tonto*
	Albert Finney, *Murder on the Orient Express*
	Dustin Hoffman, *Lenny*
	Jack Nicholson, *Chinatown*
	Al Pacino, *The Godfather, Part II*
Actress	* Ellen Burstyn, *Alice Doesn't Live Here Anymore*
	Diahann Carroll, *Claudine*
	Faye Dunaway, *Chinatown*
	Valerie Perrine, *Lenny*
	Gena Rowlands, *A Woman Under the Influence*
Supporting Actor	Fred Astaire, *The Towering Inferno*
	Jeff Bridges, *Thunderbolt and Lightfoot*
	* Robert De Niro, *The Godfather, Part II*
	Michael V. Gazzo, *The Godfather, Part II*
	Lee Strasberg, *The Godfather, Part II*
Supporting Actress	* Ingrid Bergman, *Murder on the Orient Express*
	Valentina Cortese, *Day For Night*
	Madeline Kahn, *Blazing Saddles*
	Diane Ladd, *Alice Doesn't Live Here Anymore*
	Talia Shire, *The Godfather, Part II*

Left: Francis Ford Coppola, Best Director, *The Godfather, Part II.* *Right:* Best Screenplay winner for *Chinatown,* Robert Towne.

Original Screenplay: Robert Towne, *Chinatown*

Adapted Screenplay: Francis Ford Coppola and Mario Puzo, *The Godfather, Part II*

Foreign Film: *Amarcord,* Italy, Federico Fellini

Cinematography: Fred Koenekamp and Joseph Biroc, *The Towering Inferno*

Editing: Harold F. Kress and Carl Kress, *The Towering Inferno*

Score: (original dramatic score) Nino Rota and Carmine Coppola, *The Godfather, Part II*
(original song score and/or adaptation) Nelson Riddle, *The Great Gatsby*

Original Song: "We May Never Love Like This Again," *The Towering Inferno,* Al Kasha and Joel Hirschhorn

Art Direction: Dean Tavoularis and Angelo Graham, *The Godfather, Part II*

Costume Design: Theoni V. Aldredge, *The Great Gatsby*

Sound: Ronald Pierce and Melvin Metcalfe, Sr., *Earthquake*

Visual Effects: Frank Brendel, Glen Robinson and Albert Whitlock, *Earthquake*

Short films: (animated) "Closed Mondays"
(live action) "One–Eyed Men Are Kings"

Documentary: (feature) "Hearts and Minds"
   (short) "Don't"

Thalberg Award: Not given this year

Jean Hersholt Humanitarian Award: Arthur B. Krim

Honorary Oscar®: Howard Hawks.
   Jean Renoir.

Francis Ford Coppola's Oscars® for the *The Godfather, Part II* were somehow inevitable—after all, in 1974, he co–wrote and directed it, wrote and directed *The Conversation*—which won the Palme D'Or at the Cannes Film Festival—and wrote the script for *The Great Gatsby*, the latter an aesthetic crime which Hollywood forgave.

Bert Schneider, co–producer of the Oscar®-winning documentary, *Heart and Minds*, read a telegram of congratulations from the Viet Cong delegation at the Paris Peace talks. After furious arguments backstage, Frank Sinatra came out to read a disclaimer against the telegram.

In the wonderful world of bizarre coincidences, Best Actor Art Carney and Best Actress Ellen Burstyn (who appeared as Carney's daughter in *Harry and Tonto*) had both worked with Jackie Gleason on his TV show. Burstyn couldn't make it to the Oscars®, so her director, Martin Scorsese, accepted for her. This is the closest that Scorsese has come to winning an Oscar®.

For the first time at the Academy Awards®, television had an impact in the competition itself. Where the studios and producers had in the past concentrated on buying advertisements in the "Bible of Show Business," *Variety*, and in holding deluxe private screenings, 20th Century–Fox pointed out that Academy members could see *Claudine*, which had flopped badly in the spring, on L.A.'s cable movie station, Z Channel. Given the complaints, then as now, about the shortage of good women's roles in Hollywood movies, it is no surprise that Diahann Carroll picked up a nomination. Given the competition—Dunaway, Burstyn, Rowlands—it is no surprise that she lost.

1975

Picture	*Barry Lyndon*
	Dog Day Afternoon
	Jaws
	Nashville
	* *One Flew Over the Cuckoo's Nest*
Director	Robert Altman, *Nashville*
	Federico Fellini, *Amarcord*
	* Milos Forman, *One Flew Over the Cuckoo's Nest*
	Stanley Kubrick, *Barry Lyndon*
	Sidney Lumet, *Dog Day Afternoon*
Actor	Walter Matthau, *The Sunshine Boys*
	* Jack Nicholson, *One Flew Over the Cuckoo's Nest*
	Al Pacino, *Dog Day Afternoon*
	Maximilian Schell, *The Man in the Glass Booth*
	James Whitmore, *Give 'em Hell, Harry!*
Actress	Isabelle Adjani, *The Story of Adele H*
	Ann–Margret, *Tommy*
	* Louise Fletcher, *One Flew Over the Cuckoo's Nest*
	Glenda Jackson, *Hedda*
	Carol Kane, *Hester Street*
Supporting Actor	* George Burns, *The Sunshine Boys*
	Brad Dourif, *One Flew Over the Cuckoo's Nest*
	Burgess Meredith, *The Day of the Locust*
	Chris Sarandon, *Dog Day Afternoon*
	Jack Warden, *Shampoo*
Supporting Actress	Ronee Blakley, *Nashville*
	* Lee Grant, *Shampoo*
	Sylvia Miles, *Farewell, My Lovely*
	Lily Tomlin, *Nashville*
	Brenda Vaccaro, *Jacqueline Susann's Once Is Not Enough*

Original Screenplay: Frank Pierson, *Dog Day Afternoon*

Left: Jack Nicholson, Best Actor, in *One Flew Over the Cuckoo's Nest. Right:* Best Editing Oscar® winner, *Jaws.*

Adapted Screenplay: Lawrence Hauben and Bo Goldman, *One Flew Over the Cuckoo's Nest*

Foreign Film: *Dersu Uzala*, Japan–Russia, Akira Kurosawa

Cinematography: John Alcott, *Barry Lyndon*

Editing: Verna Fields, *Jaws*

Score: (original score) John Williams, *Jaws*
(original song score and/or adaptation) Leonard Rosenman, *Barry Lyndon*

Original Song: "I'm Easy," *Nashville*, Keith Carradine

Art Direction: Ken Adam and Roy Walker, *Barry Lyndon*

Costume Design: Ulla-Britt Soderlund and Milena Canonero, *Barry Lyndon*

Sound: Robert L. Hoyt, Roger Heman, Earl Madery and John Carter, *Jaws*

Sound Effects: Peter Berkos, *The Hindenburg*

Visual Effects: Albert Whitlock and Glen Robinson, *The Hindenburg*

Short films: (animated) "Great"
(live action) "Angel and Big Joe"

Documentary: (feature) *The Man Who Skied Down Mount Everest*
(short) "The End of the Game"

Thalberg Award: Mervyn LeRoy

Jean Hersholt Humanitarian Award: Jules C. Stein

Honorary Oscar®: Mary Pickford.

For the second time in Oscar® history, a single film swept the big five—Picture, Director, Screenplay and both acting awards. If *It Happened One Night* was driven by its sheer star power, and *Silence of the Lambs* by what one suspects were very narrow victories in very strong acting categories, one suspects that *One Flew Over the Cuckoo's Nest* got its sweep through the sheer weirdness of the Best Actress category—a French ingenue (Isabelle Adjani), Ann–Margret in an oddball rock movie, an American ingenue in a tiny independent movie (Carol Kane), two–time winner Glenda Jackson, and Louise Fletcher in *Cuckoo's Nest*—a role which is technically a lead but actually a supporting performance. Ellen Burstyn was so incensed by the absence of strong women's roles that she suggested that the academy membership boycott the category in protest.

One also wonders if *Cuckoo's Nest*'s sweep was in part a cumulative award for Nicholson, who had been nominated the two years previous for *The Last Detail* and *Chinatown* without winning Oscars® that many felt he deserved. One might make the same argument for Faye Dunaway's Oscar® the next year, that it was as much for *Chinatown* as it was for *Network*.

Z channel strikes again—Maximilian Schell and James Whitmore's nominations were for films which were essentially filmed plays (Whitmore's, especially) that, aside from their Oscar® qualifying run in L.A. theatres, went straight to cable television just around nominating time.

1976

Picture	*All The President's Men* *Bound for Glory* *Network* * *Rocky* *Taxi Driver*
Director	*John G. Avildsen, *Rocky* Ingmar Bergman, *Face to Face* Sidney Lumet, *Network* Alan J. Pakula, *All the President's Men* Lina Wertmuller, *Seven Beauties*
Actor	Robert De Niro, *Taxi Driver* * Peter Finch, *Network* Giancarlo Giannini, *Seven Beauties* William Holden, *Network* Sylvester Stallone, *Rocky*
Actress	Marie–Christine Barrault, *Cousin, Cousine* * Faye Dunaway, *Network* Talia Shire, *Rocky* Sissy Spacek, *Carrie* Liv Ullman, *Face to Face*
Supporting Actor	Ned Beatty, *Network* Burgess Meredith, *Rocky* Laurence Olivier, *Marathon Man* * Jason Robards, *All the President's Men* Burt Young, *Rocky*
Supporting Actress	Jane Alexander, *All the President's Men* Jodie Foster, *Taxi Driver* Lee Grant, *Voyage of the Damned* Piper Laurie, *Carrie* * Beatrice Straight, *Network*

Original Screenplay: Paddy Chayefsky, *Network*

Adapted Screenplay: William Goldman, *All the President's Men*

Foreign Film: *Black and White in Color*, Ivory Coast, Jean–Jacques Annaud

Cinematography: Haskell Wexler, *Bound For Glory*

Left: Jason Robards, Best Supporting Actor, *All The President's Men. Right:* Best Actor Peter Finch, with co-star Faye Dunaway, in *Network.*

Editing: Richard Halsey and Scott Conrad, *Rocky*

Score: (original) Jerry Goldsmith, *The Omen*
    (song score or adaptation score) Leonard Rosenman,
      Bound For Glory

Original Song: "Evergreen," *A Star is Born*, Barbra Streisand,
    music, Paul Williams, lyrics

Art Direction: George Jenkins, *All the President's Men*

Costume Design: Danilo Donati, *Fellini's Casanova*

Sound: Arthur Piantadosi, Les Fresholtz, Dick Alexander and
    Jim Webb, *All the President's Men*

Short films: (animated) "Leisure"
    (live action) "In the Region of Ice"

Documentary: (feature) *Harlan County, U.S.A.*
    (short) "Number Our Days"

Visual Effects: Carlo Rambaldi, Glen Robinson and Frank
    Van Der Veer, *King Kong*
    L.B. Abbott, Glen Robinson and Matthew Yuricich,
    Logan's Run

Thalberg Award: Pandro S. Berman

Jean Hersholt Humanitarian Award: Not given

If 1956 has the worst assortment of Best Picture nominees, 1976 may have the best—there are no duds among this group. Although the Hollywood Establishment dislikes the Awards Show intensely, my memories of it, under director William Friedkin, was of a brisk, well-paced show that actually finished on time.

Sylvester Stallone may have worn out much of his welcome among filmgoers, but the first *Rocky* is still terrific, in part because of Stallone's freshness as a performer and in part because director John Avildsen, for whom *Rocky* is a career-crowning moment, does not indulge his star. Several critics have noted that the most remarkable thing about *Rocky* in comparison with its sequels, is how few closeups are in the film. "There don't seem to be enough real men to go around," was Stallone's explanation of *Rocky*'s success.

Network dominated the acting nominations—five nominations, three wins, including the first posthumous acting prize to Peter Finch, who had died at the Beverly Hills Hotel in January. In light of the confusion around the size of roles and how they are categorized, supporting actress Beatrice Straight had ten minutes of screen time in *Network*, roughly 10% of Tatum O'Neal's supporting actress turn in *Paper Moon*. Ned Beatty, when asked what advice he would give to young actors, said "take whatever work you can get. Never be too proud to turn down small parts. I had one day's work on *Network*, and got an Oscar® nomination."

Most memorable acceptance speech: The vertically challenged Paul Williams, co-winner of Best Song with Barbra Streisand, said "I was going to thank all the little people, but then I remembered I am the little people."

Alert the media: Lina Wertmuller becomes the first woman ever nominated as Best Director. Piper Laurie set some kind of record with her nomination as Best Supporting Actress for *Carrie*—it was her second consecutive Oscar® nomination. Her previous nomination was for the film she made before *Carrie*—*The Hustler*, in 1961.

1977

Picture	*Annie Hall*
	The Goodbye Girl
	Julia
	Star Wars
	The Turning Point
Director	*Woody Allen, *Annie Hall*
	George Lucas, *Star Wars*
	Herbert Ross, *The Turning Point*
	Steven Spielberg, *Close Encounters of the Third Kind*
	Fred Zinneman, *Julia*
Actor	*Woody Allen, *Annie Hall*
	Richard Burton, *Equus*
	*Richard Dreyfuss, *The Goodbye Girl*
	Marcello Mastroianni, *A Special Day*
	John Travolta, *Saturday Night Fever*
Actress	Anne Bancroft, *The Turning Point*
	Jane Fonda, *Julia*
	*Diane Keaton, *Annie Hall*
	Shirley MacLaine, *The Turning Point*
	Marsha Mason, *The Goodbye Girl*
Supporting Actor	Mikhail Baryshnikov, *The Turning Point*
	Peter Firth, *Equus*
	Alec Guinness, *Star Wars*
	*Jason Robards, *Julia*
	Maximilian Schell, *Julia*
Supporting Actress	Leslie Browne, *The Turning Point*
	Quinn Cummings, *The Goodbye Girl*
	Melinda Dillon, *Close Encounters of the Third Kind*
	*Vanessa Redgrave, *Julia*
	Tuesday Weld, *Looking for Mr. Goodbar*

Original Screenplay: Woody Allen, Marshall Brickman, *Annie Hall*

Adapted Screenplay: Alvin Sargent, *Julia*

Foreign Film: *Madame Rosa*, French, Moshe Mizrahi

Left: Woody Allen, Best Director/Best Picture, *Annie Hall. Right:* Best Actor Richard Dreyfuss in *The Goodbye Girl.*

Cinematography: Vilmos Zsigmond, *Close Encounters of the Third Kind*

Editing: Paul Hirsch, Marcia Lucas, and Richard Chew, *Star Wars*

Score: (original) John Williams, *Star Wars*
(song score/adaptation score) Jonathan Tunick, *A Little Night Music*

Original Song: "You Light Up My Life," *You Light Up My Life,* Joseph Brooks

Art Direction: John Barry, Norman Reynolds and Leslie Dilley, *Star Wars*

Costume Design: John Mollo, *Star Wars*

Sound: Don MacDougall, Ray West, Bob Minkler and Derek Ball, *Star Wars*

Visual Effects: John Stears, John Dykstra, Richard Edlund, Grant McCune and Robert Black, *Star Wars*

Short film: (animated) "Sand Castle"
(live action) "I'll Find A Way"

Documentary: (feature) *Who Are the Debolts? And Where Did They Get Nineteen Kids?*
(short) "Gravity is My Enemy"

Thalberg Award: Walter Mirisch

Jean Hersholt Humanitarian Award: Charlton Heston

Special Achievement Awards: Frank Warner, Sound Effects
editing, *Close Encounters of the Third Kind*
Ben Burtt, for sound effects, *Star Wars*

Honorary Oscar®: Margaret Booth, editor.
Gordon E. Sawyer and Sidney Salkow, for service to the
Academy.

Do we remember 1977 as the *Annie Hall* Oscars®, where Woody
Allen didn't show up—he never has—or do we remember it as the
year that Best Supporting Actress winner Vanessa Redgrave
made her response to the Jewish Defense League's protests
against her nomination—she favored a Palestinian homeland—
with remarks about Hollywood's courage in resisting "Zionist
hoodlums." Of course, Hollywood exploded, and it fell to Paddy
Chayefsky, presenting the writing awards, to go on stage and
denounce Redgrave for subverting the Oscars® with her politics.
Redgrave did have her defenders, most notably the winner of the
best foreign film Oscar®, Israeli director Moshe Mizrahi.

With all the furor over Redgrave—who showed up, accepted
her Oscar®, and made rather a gracious speech commending the
Academy on its courage—no one said boo about Woody Allen,
who, over the years, has never acknowledged his many Oscar®
nominations as writer and director, never attended the Oscars®,
and described the Academy Awards® as "meaningless." In his
own way, he's as recalcitrant as George C. Scott.

Nominations are one thing, but four Oscars®? During nomination and voting time, *Annie Hall* began playing in L.A. on—you
guessed it—Z Channel.

1978

Picture	*Coming Home*
	* *The Deer Hunter*
	Heaven Can Wait
	Midnight Express
	An Unmarried Woman
Director	Woody Allen, *Interiors*
	Hal Ashby, *Coming Home*
	Warren Beatty and Buck Henry, *Heaven Can Wait*
	* Michael Cimino, *The Deer Hunter*
	Alan Parker, *Midnight Express*
Actor	Warren Beatty, *Heaven Can Wait*
	Gary Busey, *The Buddy Holly Story*
	Robert De Niro, *The Deer Hunter*
	Laurence Olivier, *The Boys from Brazil*
	* Jon Voight, *Coming Home*
Actress	Ingrid Bergman, *Autumn Sonata*
	Ellen Burstyn, *Same Time, Next Year*
	Jill Clayburgh, *An Unmarried Woman*
	* Jane Fonda, *Coming Home*
	Geraldine Page, *Interiors*
Supporting Actor	Bruce Dern, *Coming Home*
	Richard Farnsworth, *Comes a Horseman*
	John Hurt, *Midnight Express*
	* Christopher Walken, *The Deer Hunter*
	Jack Warden, *Heaven Can Wait*
Supporting Actress	Dyan Cannon, *Heaven Can Wait*
	Penelope Milford, *Coming Home*
	* Maggie Smith, *California Suite*
	Maureen Stapleton, *Interiors*
	Meryl Streep, *The Deer Hunter*

Original Screenplay: Waldo Salt, Robert C. Jones, Nancy Dowd, *Coming Home*

Adapted Screenplay: Oliver Stone, *Midnight Express*

Foreign Film: *Get Out Your Handkerchiefs*, France, Bertrand Blier

Left: Christopher Walken, Best Supporting Actor, *The Deer Hunter. Right:* Bertrand Blier, Best Foreign Film Director, *Get Out Your Handkerchiefs.*

Cinematography: Nestor Almendros, *Days of Heaven*

Editing: Peter Zinner, *The Deer Hunter*

Score: (original score) Giorgio Moroder, *Midnight Express*
(song score or adaptation score) Joe Renzetti, *The Buddy Holly Story*

Original Song: "Last Dance," *Thank God It's Friday*, Paul Jabara

Art Direction: Paul Sylbert and Edwin O'Donovan, *Heaven Can Wait*

Costume Design: Anthony Powell, *Death on the Nile*

Sound: Richard Portman, William McCaughey, Aaron Rochin and Darrin Knight, *The Deer Hunter*

Visual Effects: Les Bowie, Colin Chilvers, Denys Coop, Roy Field, Derek Meddings, Zoran Perisic, *Superman*

Short films: (animated) "Special Delivery"
(live action) "Teenage Father"

Documentary: (feature) *Scared Straight!*
(short) "The Flight of the Gossamer Condor"

Thalberg Award: Not given

Jean Hersholt Humanitarian Award: Leo Jaffe

Honorary Oscar®: Walter Lantz, creator of Woody
   Woodpecker.
   Laurence Olivier.
   King Vidor.
   The Museum of Modern Art Film Department.

Rule Changes: The Special Effects category became a "special
achievement award," rather than a regular category.

Four years after the fall of Saigon and the end of the Vietnam
War, it was felt safe for Hollywood to use Vietnam as a dramatic
setting. So, at the 1978 Academy Awards®, viewers were presented with the simultaneous surreal and touching image of a
gaunt, plainly–ill John Wayne presenting the Best Picture award
on an evening devoted to honoring films that he probably hated—
Coming Home and *The Deer Hunter*, Hollywood's first wave of
anti–Vietnam films. For *The Deer Hunter*, the film was positioned
to make the Oscars® a part of their marketing campaign—the film
had only played a week in New York and L.A. in December. Its
real opening was slated to take advantage of the critics' awards
and Oscar® nominations.

When the three writers who had contributed to *Coming Home*
stood on the stage of the Dorothy Chandler Pavilion to accept
their Oscars®, the world had the interesting experience of seeing
three people who had collaborated on a screenplay without actually meeting. Nancy Dowd's original script had been commis-
sioned by Jane Fonda in 1973. Later in the evening, when Fonda
received her Oscar® as Best Actress, Dowd was not among those
she thanked. Fonda, for her part, led a campaign against *The Deer
Hunter*. She hadn't seen it, but friends had told her that it was
racist—in the post–awards press scrum, when asked about
Cimino's film, she said "I still haven't seen it, but ours is the best
picture."

Laurence Olivier, honored with a special Oscar® for his career
of achievements, attended for the first time since 1939, and deliv-
ered a speech that defied comprehension, but sounded wonderful.
The evening's best one–liner, however, came from Shirley Mac-
Laine, who talked about how proud she was of brother Warren
Beatty, then mused "Imagine what you could accomplish if you
tried celibacy."

1979

Picture	*All That Jazz* *Apocalypse Now* *Breaking Away* * *Kramer vs. Kramer* *Norma Rae*
Director	*Robert Benton, *Kramer vs. Kramer* Francis Ford Coppola, *Apocalypse Now* Bob Fosse, *All That Jazz* Edouard Molinaro, *La Cage Aux Folles* Peter Yates, *Breaking Away*
Actor	*Dustin Hoffman, *Kramer vs. Kramer* Jack Lemmon, *The China Syndrome* Al Pacino, *And Justice for All* Roy Scheider, *All That Jazz* Peter Sellers, *Being There*
Actress	Jill Clayburgh, *Starting Over* * Sally Field, *Norma Rae* Jane Fonda, *The China Syndrome* Marsha Mason, *Chapter Two* Bette Midler, *The Rose*
Supporting Actor	*Melvyn Douglas, *Being There* Robert Duvall, *Apocalypse Now* Frederic Forrest, *The Rose* Justin Henry, *Kramer vs. Kramer* Mickey Rooney, *The Black Stallion*
Supporting Actress	Jane Alexander, *Kramer vs. Kramer* Barbara Barrie, *Breaking Away* Candice Bergen, *Starting Over* Mariel Hemingway, *Manhattan* * Meryl Streep, *Kramer vs. Kramer*

Original Screenplay: Steve Tesich, *Breaking Away*

Adapted Screenplay: Robert Benton, *Kramer vs. Kramer*

Foreign Film: *The Tin Drum*, Germany, Volcker Schlondorff

Cinematography: Vittorio Storaro, *Apocalypse Now*

Editing: Alan Heim, *All That Jazz*

Left: Meryl Streep and Dustin Hoffman with director Robert Benton in Best Picture, *Kramer vs. Kramer. Right:* Meryle Streep, Best Supporting Actress, *Kramer vs. Kramer.*

Score: (original score) Georges Delerue, *A Little Romance*
(original song score or adaptation score) Ralph Burns, *All That Jazz*

Original Song: "It Goes Like it Goes," *Norma Rae,* David Shire, music, Norman Gimbel, lyrics

Art Direction: Philip Rosenberg and Tony Walton, *All That Jazz*

Costume Design: Albert Wolsky, *All That Jazz*

Visual Effects: H.R. Giger, Carlo Rambaldi, Brian Johnson, Nick Allder and Denys Ayling, *Alien*

Sound: Walter Murch, *Apocalypse Now*

Short films: (animated) "Every Child"
(live action) "Board and Care"

Documentary: (feature) *Best Boy*
(short) "Paul Robeson, Tribute to an Artist"

Thalberg Award: Ray Stark

Jean Hersholt Humanitarian Award: Robert Benjamin

Honorary Oscar®: Hal Elias, for distinguished service to the Academy.
Alec Guinness.

Special Achievement Award: Alan Splet, sound editing, *The Black Stallion*

Rule Change: The special Visual Effects category became a competitive award—again.

One of the most predictable Academy Awards® in history: Dustin Hoffman and Sally Field had won every critics' award, industry citation and Golden Globe available to them for their performances in *Kramer vs. Kramer* and *Norma Rae*. These were roles that neither actor actually wanted. Field took *Norma Rae* on the advice of Burt Reynolds after Jill Clayburgh, Jane Fonda and Faye Dunaway all turned it down. Hoffman only agreed to do the film after demanding more rewrites, the right to improvise, and access to the cutting room. The ceremony itself seemed a bit of an afterthought—by the way, this is not the year of Field's famous "You really like me" speech. That came in '84 when, coincidentally, her director was *Kramer*'s Robert Benton.

Robert Benton became the latest writer–director to win both Oscars® for a single film, and somehow managed to trip on both his trips to the podium. Howard Koch complained about Ira Wohl, the documentary feature winner for *Best Boy*, whose acceptance speech lasted for four minutes. On the other hand, Dustin Hoffman's speech lasted a minute longer, and nobody complained. Hoffman talked about all the actors in the Screen Actors' Guild who don't get to work, and how he doesn't believe that he beat his competition. There is no evidence that he put the statue on display at the SAG offices, or had the names of his competition engraved on it. To liven up the proceedings, Meryl Streep left her Oscar® in the ladies' room.

Picture	*Coal Miner's Daughter* *The Elephant Man* **Ordinary People* *Raging Bull* *Tess*
Director	David Lynch, *The Elephant Man* Roman Polanski, *Tess* *Robert Redford, *Ordinary People* Richard Rush, *The Stunt Man* Martin Scorsese, *Raging Bull*
Actor	*Robert De Niro, *Raging Bull* Robert Duvall, *The Great Santini* John Hurt, *The Elephant Man* Jack Lemmon, *Tribute* Peter O'Toole, *The Stunt Man*
Actress	Ellen Burstyn, *Resurrection* Goldie Hawn, *Private Benjamin* Mary Tyler Moore, *Ordinary People* Gena Rowlands, *Gloria* *Sissy Spacek, *Coal Miner's Daughter*
Supporting Actor	Judd Hirsch, *Ordinary People* *Timothy Hutton, *Ordinary People* Michael O'Keefe, *The Great Santini* Joe Pesci, *Raging Bull* Jason Robards, *Melvin and Howard*
Supporting Actress	Eileen Brennan, *Private Benjamin* Eva La Gallienne, *Resurrection* Cathy Moriarty, *Raging Bull* Diana Scarwid, *Inside Moves* *Mary Steenburgen, *Melvin and Howard*

Original Screenplay: Bo Goldman, *Melvin and Howard*

Adapted Screenplay: Alvin Sargent, *Ordinary People*

Foreign Film: *Moscow Does Not Believe in Tears*, Russia, Vladimir Menshov

Cinematography: Geoffrey Unsworth, Ghislaine Cloquet, *Tess*

Editing: Thelma Schoonmaker, *Raging Bull*

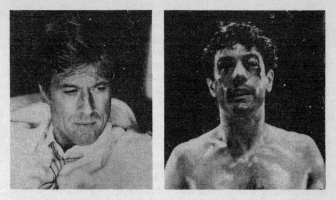

Left: Robert Redford, Best Director, *Ordinary People. Right:* Best Actor Robert De Niro in *Raging Bull.*

Score: Michael Gore, *Fame*

Original Song: "Fame," Michael Gore, music, Dean Pitchford, lyrics

Art Direction: Pierre Guffroy and Jack Stevens, *Tess*

Costume Design: Anthony Powell, *Tess*

Sound: Bill Varney, Steve Maslow, Greg Landaker and Peter Sutton, *The Empire Strikes Back*

Visual Effects: Brian Johnson, Richard Edlund, Denis Muren and Bruce Nicholson, *The Empire Strikes Back*

Short films: (animated) "The Fly"
(live action) "The Dollar Bottom"

Documentary: (feature) *From Mao to Mozart: Isaac Stern in China*
(short) "Karl Hess: Toward Liberty"

Thalberg Award: Not given

Jean Hersholt Humanitarian Award: Not given

Honorary Oscar®: Henry Fonda.

Rule Changes: The Special Visual Effects category was changed back to a "special achievement award." Original score became the only competition for score.

In the late '70s and early '80s, there was a popular television show called "Real People." At the Oscars® in 1980, that title was taken to heart—three of the four acting awards went to actors playing real people, and not historical figures, either, but living breathing people who were around to critique their performances. Sissy Spacek was hand-picked by Loretta Lynn for *Coal Miner's Daughter*, and Robert De Niro trained under the eye of Jake LaMotta, whom he would play in *Raging Bull*. LaMotta's younger brother, Joey, decided to sue Scorsese and United Artists because he disliked the way Joe Pesci played him. De Niro's acceptance speech thank-you list included Joey LaMotta, "even though he's suing us."

The actual Awards show was delayed for 24 hours because of the shooting of Ronald Reagan by John Hinckley, a great admirer of nominated director Martin Scorsese and future Oscar® winner Jodie Foster. The president's fragile condition didn't protect him from Johnny Carson's opening monologue, though. Carson described Reagan's request for cuts in arts funding as "Reagan's strongest attack on the arts since he signed with Warner Brothers."

They are rich, powerful, indecently attractive, but what they really want is to direct. Robert Redford and Warren Beatty win back-to-back Best Direction Oscars®—and Director's Guild Awards—for *Ordinary People* and *Reds*. Michael Jackson and Diana Ross came to the ceremonies together.

1981

Picture	*Atlantic City*
	* *Chariots of Fire*
	On Golden Pond
	Raiders of the Lost Ark
	Reds
Director	*Warren Beatty, *Reds*
	Hugh Hudson, *Chariots of Fire*
	Louis Malle, *Atlantic City*
	Mark Rydell, *On Golden Pond*
	Steven Spielberg, *Raiders of the Lost Ark*
Actor	Warren Beatty, *Reds*
	* Henry Fonda, *On Golden Pond*
	Burt Lancaster, *Atlantic City*
	Dudley Moore, *Arthur*
	Paul Newman, *Absence of Malice*
Actress	*Katharine Hepburn, *On Golden Pond*
	Diane Keaton, *Reds*
	Marsha Mason, *Only When I Laugh*
	Susan Sarandon, *Atlantic City*
	Meryl Streep, *The French Lieutenant's Woman*
Supporting Actor	James Coco, *Only When I Laugh*
	*John Gielgud, *Arthur*
	Ian Holm, *Chariots of Fire*
	Jack Nicholson, *Reds*
	Howard E. Rollins, *Ragtime*
Supporting Actress	Melinda Dillon, *Absence of Malice*
	Jane Fonda, *On Golden Pond*
	Joan Hackett, *Only When I Laugh*
	Elizabeth McGovern, *Ragtime*
	*Maureen Stapleton, *Reds*

Original Screenplay: Colin Welland, *Chariots of Fire*

Adapted Screenplay: Ernest Thompson, *On Golden Pond*

Foreign Film: *Mephisto*, Hungary, Istvan Szabo

Cinematography: Vittorio Storaro, *Reds*

Editing: Michael Kahn, *Raiders of the Lost Ark*

Above: Best Picture, *Chariots of Fire. Right:*
Best Director Warren Beatty in *Reds.*

Score: Vangelis, *Chariots of Fire*

Original Song: "Arthur's Theme (Best That You Can Do),"
Arthur, Burt Bacharach, Carole Bayer Sager, Christopher
Cross and Peter Allen

Art Direction: Norman Reynolds and Leslie Dilley, *Raiders of
the Lost Ark*

Costume Design: Milena Canonero, *Chariots of Fire*

Makeup: Rick Baker, *An American Werewolf in London*

Sound: Bill Varney, Steve Maslow, Gregg Landaker and Roy
Charman, *Raiders of the Lost Ark*

Visual Effects: Richard Edlund, Kit West, Bruce Nicholson,
Joe Johnston, *Raiders of the Lost Ark*

Short films: (animated) "Crac"
(live action) "Violet"

Documentary: (feature) *Genocide*
(short) "Close Harmony"

Special Achievement Award: Benjamin Burtt and Richard L. Anderson, Sound Effects Editing, *Raiders of the Lost Ark*

Thalberg Award: Albert Broccoli

Jean Hersholt Humanitarian Award: Danny Kaye

Honorary Oscar®: Barbara Stanwyck.

Rule Change: Special Visual Effects became a competitive category once again.

In keeping with the popularity of *On Golden Pond*, the Academy honored the oldest collection of acting winners ever—72–year–old Katharine Hepburn, 77–year–old John Gielgud, 77–year–old Henry Fonda, and 56–year–old Maureen Stapleton—an average age of 70½ years per Oscar® winner.

The big story, however, was the war of words between pugnacious Brit producer David Puttnam, whose Cinderella winner *Chariots of Fire*, took the prizes that were expected to accrue to Warren Beatty's $50 million epic, *Reds*. (Oddly, both Beatty and Puttnam made the same argument to their friends before the Awards show—whoever wins Best Costume wins Best Picture—and they were right.)

It was an evening high on sentiment. There were all those aging actors getting awards—Maureen Stapleton had the good sense to thank "Everyone I've ever met in my entire life," Katharine Hepburn and John Gielgud didn't show up, and Jane Fonda accepted for her father and spoke for four minutes. But sentimentally speaking, the high point of the evening was the Honorary Oscar® for Barbara Stanwyck, who, on the verge of tears, dedicated it to her friend William Holden, recently deceased. The comic high point was Bette Midler, presenting the awards for best song.

Picture	E.T.—The Extraterrestrial
	Gandhi
	Missing
	Tootsie
	The Verdict
Director	*Richard Attenborough, *Gandhi*
	Sindey Lumet, *The Verdict*
	Wolfgang Petersen, *Das Boot*
	Sidney Pollack, *Tootsie*
	Steven Spielberg, *E.T.*
Actor	Dustin Hoffman, *Tootsie*
	*Ben Kingsley, *Gandhi*
	Jack Lemmon, *Missing*
	Paul Newman, *The Verdict*
	Peter O'Toole, *My Favorite Year*
Actress	Julie Andrews, *Victor/Victoria*
	Jessica Lange, *Frances*
	Sissy Spacek, *Missing*
	*Meryl Streep, *Sophie's Choice*
	Debra Winger, *An Officer and a Gentleman*
Supporting Actor	Charles Durning, *The Best Little Whorehouse in Texas*
	*Louis Gossett, Jr., *An Officer and a Gentleman*
	John Lithgow, *The World According to Garp*
	James Mason, *The Verdict*
	Robert Preston, *Victor/Victoria*
Supporting Actress	Glenn Close, *The World According to Garp*
	Teri Garr, *Tootsie*
	*Jessica Lange, *Tootsie*
	Kim Stanley, *Frances*
	Lesley Ann Warren, *Victor/Victoria*

Original Screenplay: John Briley, *Gandhi*

Adapted Screenplay: Costa–Gavras and Donald Stewart, *Missing*

Left: Ben Kingsley won the Best Actor Oscar® for *Ghandi. Right:* Richard Gere with Best Supporting Actor Louis Gossett, Jr. in *An Officer and a Gentleman.*

Foreign Film: *To Begin Again*, Spain, Jose Luis Garci

Cinematography: Billy Williams and Ronnie Taylor, *Gandhi*

Editing: John Bloom, *Gandhi*

Score: (original) John Williams, *E.T.*
(song score or adaptation score) Leslie Bricusse, *Victor/Victoria*

Original Song: "Up Where We Belong," *An Officer and a Gentleman*, Jack Nitzsche and Buffy Saint–Marie, music, Will Jennings, lyrics

Art Direction: Michael Seirton, *Gandhi*

Costume Design: John Mollo and Bhanu Athaiya, *Gandhi*

Makeup: *Quest For Fire*

Sound: Buzz Knudson, Robert Glass, Don Digirolamo and Gene Cantamessa, *E.T.*

Visual Effects: Carlo Rambaldi, Dennis Murren and Kenneth F. Smith, *E.T.*

Sound Effects Editing: Charles L. Campbell and Ben Burtt, *E.T.*

Short films: (animated) "Tango"
(live action) "A Shocking Accident"

Documentary: (feature) *Just Another Missing Kid*
  (short) "If You Love This Planet"

Thalberg Award: Not given

Jean Hersholt Humanitarian Award: Walter Mirisch

Honorary Oscar®: Mickey Rooney.

Rule Changes: The category for Sound Effects Editing became a competitive award. The category Song Score/Adaptation Score was restored.

A political year at the Oscars®, and a strange one. The State Department sued Universal over *Missing*, which implied that the American government was somehow involved in the overthrow of Allende in Chile. Then the Canadian short documentary "If You Love This Planet" was declared "foreign propaganda." At the ceremony itself, after Matt Dillon and Kristy McNichol mangled the names of the short film nominees and their films, Animated Short winner Zybigniew Rybczynski stepped out for a cigarette, couldn't get back in, got into a scuffle with a security guard, got arrested, and got bailed out by Hollywood divorce attorney Marvin Mitchelson.

On a positive note, Louis Gossett, Jr., became the first black actor to win Supporting Actor, and the first black acting winner since Sidney Poitier in 1963.

That was the good stuff. The rest of the evening was *Gandhi, Gandhi, Gandhi*, which led to some tedious speechmaking about how voting for *Gandhi* was a gesture in support of world peace. This culminated in Sir Richard Attenborough's obsequious speech on how the Academy hadn't supported him, but *Gandhi* and his pacifist vision. (*Village Voice* critic Andrew Sarris dubbed Attenborough "The Wizard of Ooze" in honor of the speech.)

Glenn Close, in her film debut, gets the first of five nominations in a decade, without winning. Thelma Ritter, nominated six times without winning, had best look to her laurels.

Best acceptance speech: Documentary short director Terri Nash, who remarked that "You sure know how to show a foreign agent a good time," and thanked the State Department for its efforts in promoting her film.

1983

Picture	*The Big Chill*
	The Dresser
	The Right Stuff
	Tender Mercies
	* *Terms of Endearment*
Director	Bruce Beresford, *Tender Mercies*
	Ingmar Bergman, *Fanny and Alexander*
	*James L. Brooks, *Terms of Endearment*
	Mike Nichols, *Silkwood*
	Peter Yates, *The Dresser*
Actor	Michael Caine, *Educating Rita*
	Tom Conti, *Reuben, Reuben*
	Tom Courtenay, *The Dresser*
	*Robert Duvall, *Tender Mercies*
	Albert Finney, *The Dresser*
Actress	Jane Alexander, *Testament*
	*Shirley MacLaine, *Terms of Endearment*
	Meryl Streep, *Silkwood*
	Julie Walters, *Educating Rita*
	Debra Winger, *Terms of Endearment*
Supporting Actor	Charles Durning, *To Be Or Not to Be*
	John Lithgow, *Terms of Endearment*
	*Jack Nicholson, *Terms of Endearment*
	Sam Shepard, *The Right Stuff*
	Rip Torn, *Cross Creek*
Supporting Actress	Cher, *Silkwood*
	Glenn Close, *The Big Chill*
	*Linda Hunt, *The Year of Living Dangerously*
	Amy Irving, *Yentl*
	Alfre Woodward, *Cross Creek*

Original Screenplay: Horton Foote, *Tender Mercies*

Adapted Screenplay: James L. Brooks, *Terms of Endearment*

Foreign Film: *Fanny & Alexander*, Sweden, Ingmar Bergman

Cinematography: Sven Nykvist, *Fanny & Alexander*

Left: Jack Nicholson, Best Supporting Actor, *Terms of Endearment. Right:* Best Supporting Actress nominee Amy Irving in *Yentl.*

Editing: Glenn Farr, Lisa Fruchtman, Stephen A. Rotter, Tom Rolf and Douglas Steward, *The Right Stuff*

Score: (original) Bill Conti, *The Right Stuff*
 (song score or adaptation) Michel Legrand, Alan and Marilyn Bergman, *Yentl*

Original Song: "Flashdance . . . What a Feeling," *Flashdance,* Giorgio Moroder, music, Keith Forsev and Irene Cara, lyrics

Art Direction: Anna Asp, *Fanny & Alexander*

Costume Design: Marik Vos, *Fanny & Alexander*

Makeup: Not given

Sound: Mark Berger, Tom Scott, Randy Thorn and David MacMillan, *The Right Stuff*

Sound Effects Editing: Jay Broeckelheide, *The Right Stuff*

Visual Effects: Richard Edlund, Dennis Muren, Ken Ralston, Phil Tippett, *Return of the Jedi*

Short films: (animated) "Sundae in New York"
 (live action): "Boys and Girls"

Documentary: (feature) *He Makes Me Feel Like Dancing*
 (short) "Flamenco at 5:15"

Thalberg Award: Not given

Jean Hersholt Humanitarian Award: Mike Frankovich

Honorary Oscar®: Hal Roach.

1982 was the year of drag performances—Julie Andrews, Dustin Hoffman, John Lithgow—but this was the year a drag performance won an Oscar®, though many people did not realize that it was a drag performance until they read the credits—Linda Hunt won for playing a Eurasian dwarf photographer in *The Year Of Living Dangerously*.

Barbra Streisand gets what she wants, or she cries foul. In 1983, she wanted *Yentl* to be nominated for Best Picture and Best Director. It wasn't, so she blamed her failure to be nominated on Hollywood's rampant sexism. She would make the same charges a decade later when *The Prince of Tides* won several nominations, but she was not nominated as director or actress.

Picture	*Amadeus*
	The Killing Fields
	A Passage to India
	Places in the Heart
	A Soldier's Story

Director	Woody Allen, *Broadway Danny Rose*
	Robert Benton, *Places in the Heart*
	*Milos Forman, *Amadeus*
	Roland Joffe, *The Killing Fields*
	David Lean, *A Passage to India*

Actor	*F. Murray Abraham, *Amadeus*
	Jeff Bridges, *Starman*
	Albert Finney, *Under the Volcano*
	Tom Hulce, *Amadeus*
	Sam Waterston, *The Killing Fields*

Actress	Judy Davis, *A Passage to India*
	*Sally Field, *Places in the Heart*
	Jessica Lange, *Country*
	Vanessa Redgrave, *The Bostonians*
	Sissy Spacek, *The River*

Supporting Actor	Adolph Caesar, *A Soldier's Story*
	John Malkovich, *Places in the Heart*
	Noriyuki "Pat" Morita, *The Karate Kid*
	*Haing S. Ngor, *The Killing Fields*
	Ralph Richardson, *Greystoke: The Legend of Tarzan, Lord of the Apes*

Supporting Actress	*Peggy Ashcroft, *A Passage to India*
	Glenn Close, *The Natural*
	Lindsay Crouse, *Places in the Heart*
	Christine Lahti, *Swing Shift*
	Geraldine Page, *The Pope of Greenwich Village*

Original Screenplay: Robert Benton, *Places in the Heart*

Adapted Screenplay: Peter Shaffer, *Amadeus*

Foreign Film: *Dangerous Moves*, Switzerland, Richard Dembo

Cinematography: Chris Menges, *The Killing Fields*

Left: Sally Field, Best Actress, *Places in the Heart. Right:* Tom Hulce and Elizabeth Berridge in Best Picture, *Amadeus.*

Editing: Jim Clark, *The Killing Fields*

Score: (original) Maurice Jarre, *A Passage to India*
    (song score) Prince, *Purple Rain*

Original Song: "I Just Called To Say I Love You," *The Woman in Red*, Stevie Wonder

Art Direction: Patrizia Von Brandenstein, *Amadeus*

Costume Design: Theodor Pistek, *Amadeus*

Makeup: Paul LeBlanc and Dick Smith, *Amadeus*

Visual Effects: Dennis Muren, Michael McAlister, Lorne Peterson and George Gibbs, *Indiana Jones and the Temple of Doom*

Sound: Mark Berger, Tom Scott, Todd Boekelheide, Chris Newman, *Amadeus*

Sound Effects Editing: Kay Rose, *The River* (Special Achievement Award)

Short films: (animated) "Charade"
    (live action) "Up"

Documentary: (feature) *The Times of Harvey Milk*
    (short) "The Stone Carvers"

Thalberg Award: Not given

Jean Hersholt Humanitarian Award: David L. Wolper

Honorary Oscar®: The National Endowment for the Arts.
James Stewart.

Maurice Jarre, who composed the score for *A Passage to India*, expressed gratitude that Mozart hadn't been eligible. Most of the nominees probably wished that all of *Amadeus* hadn't been eligible, as Milos Forman's adaptation of the Peter Schaffer play joined the Oscar® elite.

Because the Academy voters resisted the temptation, we can't actually say that the Oscars® went to the dogs in 1984. Robert Towne was so distressed by Hugh Hudson's rewrite of his *Greystoke* script that he had his name removed from the script and substituted his Writers' Guild registered pseudonym, P.H. Vazak, which is the name of his sheepdog. It's too bad—one can only dream of the acceptance speech.

After years of complaint about the composers of the Academy, that they are hidebound and conservative and completely out of touch with what people are listening to, Prince and Stevie Wonder win two of the music awards. Prince showed up in a purple limo. Stevie Wonder dedicated his award to imprisoned South African leader Nelson Mandela. South Africa promptly banned his records, which may be the first time that winning an Oscar® has adversely affected anyone's earnings.

Picture	*The Color Purple*
	Kiss of the Spider Woman
	Out of Africa *
	Prizzi's Honor
	Witness
Director	Hector Babenco, *Kiss of the Spider Woman*
	John Huston, *Prizzi's Honor*
	Akira Kurosawa, *Ran*
	*Sydney Pollack, *Out of Africa*
	Peter Weir, *Witness*
Actor	Harrison Ford, *Witness*
	James Garner, *Murphy's Romance*
	*William Hurt, *Kiss of the Spider Woman*
	Jack Nicholson, *Prizzi's Honor*
	Jon Voight, *Runaway Train*
Actress	Anne Bancroft, *Agnes of God*
	Whoopi Goldberg, *The Color Purple*
	Jessica Lange, *Sweet Dreams*
	*Geraldine Page, *The Trip to Bountiful*
	Meryl Streep, *Out of Africa*
Supporting Actor	*Don Ameche, *Cocoon*
	Klaus Maria Brandauer, *Out of Africa*
	William Hickey, *Prizzi's Honor*
	Robert Loggia, *Jagged Edge*
	Eric Roberts, *Runaway Train*
Supporting Actress	Margaret Avery, *The Color Purple*
	*Anjelica Huston, *Prizzi's Honor*
	Amy Madigan, *Twice in a Lifetime*
	Meg Tilly, *Agnes of God*
	Oprah Winfrey, *The Color Purple*

Original Screenplay: Earl W. Wallace and William Kelley, *Witness*

Adapted Screenplay: Kurt Luedtke, *Out of Africa*

Foreign Film: *The Official Story*, Argentina, Luis Puenzo

Cinematography: David Watkin, *Out of Africa*

Left: Sydney Pollack, Best Director, *Out of Africa. Right:* Anjelica Huston, Best Supporting Actress, *Prizzi's Honor.*

Editing: Thom Noble, *Witness*

Score: John Barry, *Out of Africa*

Original Song: "Say You, Say Me," *White Nights,* Lionel Richie

Art Direction: Stephen Grimes, *Out of Africa*

Costume Design: Emi Wada, *Ran*

Makeup: Michael Westmore and Zoltan Elek, *Mask*

Visual Efects: Ken Ralston, Ralph McQuarrie, Scott Farrar and David Berry, *Cocoon*

Sound: Chris Jenkins, Gary Alexander, Larry Stensvold and Peter Handford, *Out of Africa*

Sound Effects Editing: Charles L. Campbell and Robert Rutledge, *Back to the Future*

Short films: (animated) "Anna & Bella" (live action) "Molly's Pilgrim"

Documentary: (feature) *Broken Rainbow* (short) "Witness to War: Dr. Charlie Clements"

Thalberg Award: Not given

Jean Hersholt Humanitarian Award: Charles "Buddy" Rogers

Honorary Oscar®: Paul Newman.
    Alex North, composer.
    John H. Whitney, film pioneer.

The Color Purple joins *The Turning Point* as the film with the most nominations without winning an Oscar®—eleven. As a final slap in the face, Spielberg himself is not nominated.

Sydney Pollack goes to Africa to make a movie about a lady of the manor who lords it over the native help and her boyfriend, a great white hunter, and *Out of Africa* wins six Oscars®.

Michael Westmore's Makeup Oscar® for *Mask* was a family award. The Westmores were legendary for makeup in Hollywood—a Westmore did Karloff's Frankenstein makeup back in 1931, and one suspects that if there had been Makeup Oscars® for as long as there had been costume awards, the Westmores would have more Oscars® than Edith Head.

1986

Picture	*Children of a Lesser God*
	Hannah and Her Sisters
	The Mission
	* Platoon
	A Room with a View

Director   Woody Allen, *Hannah and Her Sisters*
James Ivory, *A Room with a View*
Roland Joffe, *The Mission*
David Lynch, *Blue Velvet*
* Oliver Stone, *Platoon*

Actor   Dexter Gordon, *'Round Midnight*
Bob Hoskins, *Mona Lisa*
William Hurt, *Children of a Lesser God*
* Paul Newman, *The Color of Money*
James Woods, *Salvador*

Actress   Jane Fonda, *The Morning After*
* Marlee Matlin, *Children of a Lesser God*
Sissy Spacek, *Crimes of the Heart*
Kathleen Turner, *Peggy Sue Got Married*
Sigourney Weaver, *Aliens*

Supporting Actor   Tom Berenger, *Platoon*
* Michael Caine, *Hannah and Her Sisters*
Willem Dafoe, *Platoon*
Denholm Elliott, *A Room with a View*
Dennis Hopper, *Hoosiers*

Supporting Actress   Tess Harper, *Crimes of the Heart*
Piper Laurie, *Children of a Lesser God*
Mary Elizabeth Mastrantonio, *The Color of Money*
Maggie Smith, *A Room with a View*
* Dianne Wiest, *Hannah and Her Sisters*

Original Screenplay: Woody Allen, *Hannah and Her Sisters*

Adapted Screenplay: Ruth Prawer Jhabvala, *A Room with a View*

Foreign Film: *The Assault*, Dutch, Fons Rademakers

Left: Paul Newman, Best Actor, in *The Color of Money.* *Right:* Herbie Hancock, composer of the Best Score, *'Round Midnight.*

Cinematography: Chris Menges, *The Mission*

Editing: Claire Simpson, *Platoon*

Score: Herbie Hancock, *'Round Midnight*

Original Song: "Take My Breath Away," *Top Gun,* Giorgio Moroder, music, Tom Whitlock, lyrics

Art Direction: Gianni Quaranta and Brian Ackland–Snow, *A Room with a View*

Costume Design: Jenny Beaven and John Bright, *A Room with a View*

Makeup: Chris Walas and Stephan Dupuis, *The Fly*

Visual Effects: Robert Skotak, Stan Winston, John Richardson and Suzanne Benson, *Aliens*

Sound: John Wilkinson, Richard Rodgers, Charles Grenzbach and Simon Kaye, *Platoon*

Sound Effects Editing: Don Sharpe, *Aliens*

Short films: (animated) "A Greek Tragedy" (live action) "Precious Images"

Documentary: (feature) *Down and Out in America Artie Shaw, Time is All You've Got,* (two winners) (short) "Woman—For America, For the World"

Thalberg Award: Steven Spielberg

Jean Hersholt Humanitarian Award: Not given

Honorary Oscar®: Ralph Bellamy.
    E.M. "Al" Lewis.

Going for the ultimate in realism, the Academy honored the you–are–there authenticity of Oliver Stone's grunts' eye view of the war in Vietnam, complete with paternal symbolism and the Christ figure played by Willem Dafoe. *Platoon* won Oliver Stone his second Oscar® and first of two directing Oscars®. The Academy showed extraordinary taste by giving Woody Allen the original screenplay Oscar® for *Hannah and Her Sisters*, despite the fact that Allen did not campaign and more than once expressed his distaste for the Oscars®.

For the second time in the decade, the Academy followed up an Honorary Oscar® with a competitive Oscar®, and in both cases, it was Best Actor—Henry Fonda in 1980–81, and Paul Newman for reprising his "Fast Eddie" Felson from *The Hustler* in the sequel, *The Color of Money*. The strange thing about this is that *The Color of Money* is less sequel than remake, with Felson twenty years later having turned into the evil Bert Gordon, the character George C. Scott was nominated for in 1961.

By honoring with the Irving Thalberg Memorial Award Spielberg as producer rather than a director, the Academy's Board of Governors was honoring the creative mind behind *Goonies* and *Gremlins* and *Young Sherlock Holmes* rather than the creative mind behind *Jaws* and *Raiders of the Lost Ark*.

1987

Picture	*Broadcast News*
	Fatal Attraction
	Hope and Glory
	* *The Last Emperor*
	Moonstruck
Director	*Bernardo Bertolucci, *The Last Emperor*
	John Boorman, *Hope and Glory*
	Lasse Hellstrom, *My Life as a Dog*
	Norman Jewison, *Moonstruck*
	Adrian Lyne, *Fatal Attraction*
Actor	*Michael Douglas, *Wall Street*
	William Hurt, *Broadcast News*
	Marcello Mastroianni, *Dark Eyes*
	Jack Nicholson, *Ironweed*
	Robin Williams, *Good Morning Vietnam*
Actress	*Cher, *Moonstruck*
	Glenn Close, *Fatal Attraction*
	Holly Hunter, *Broadcast News*
	Sally Kirkland, *Anna*
	Meryl Streep, *Ironweed*
Supporting Actor	Albert Brooks, *Broadcast News*
	*Sean Connery, *The Untouchables*
	Morgan Freeman, *Street Smart*
	Vincent Gardenia, *Moonstruck*
	Denzel Washington, *Cry Freedom*
Supporting Actress	Norma Aleandro, *Gaby—a True Story*
	Anne Archer, *Fatal Attraction*
	*Olympia Dukakis, *Moonstruck*
	Anne Ramsey, *Throw Momma From the Train*
	Ann Sothern, *The Whales of August*

Original Screenplay: John Patrick Shanley, *Moonstruck*

Adapted Screenplay: Mark Peploe and Bernardo Bertolucci, *The Last Emperor*

Foreign Film: *Babette's Feast*, Denmark, Gabriel Axel

Left: Michael Douglas, Best Actor, *Wall Street. Right:* Best Supporting Actor Sean Connery with Kevin Costner in *The Untouchables.*

Cinematography: Vittorio Storaro, *The Last Emperor*

Editing: Gabriella Cristiani, *The Last Emperor*

Score: Ryuichi Sakamoto, David Byrne and Cong Su, *The Last Emperor*

Original Song: "I've Had the Time of My Life," *Dirty Dancing,* Franke Previte, John DenIcola, and Donald Markowitz, music, Franke Previte, lyrics

Art Direction: Ferdinando Scarfiotti, *The Last Emperor*

Costume Design: James Acheson, *The Last Emperor*

Makeup: Rick Baker, *Harry and the Hendersons*

Sound: Bill Rowe and Ivan Sharrock, *The Last Emperor*

Sound Effects Editing: Stephen Flick and John Pospisil, *RoboCop* (Special Achievement Award)

Short films: (animated) "The Man Who Planted Trees" (live action short) "Ray's Male Heterosexual Dance Hall"

Documentary: (feature) *The Ten Year Lunch: The Wit and Legend of the Algonquin Round Table* (short) "Young At Heart"

Visual Effects: Dennis Muren, William George, Harley Jessup and Kenneth Smith, *Innerspace*

Thalberg Award: Billy Wilder

Jean Hersholt Humanitarian Award: Not given

Honorary Oscar®: None given

The 60th Anniversary Oscars® labored under a Writers' Guild strike, so the Academy turned to people who could make things up—stand-up comedians—to act as hosts and presenters. Chevy Chase opened the show "Good evening, Hollywood phonies," and Sean Connery's acceptance speech included a wish that the strike might be ended. Best of all, Robin Williams, presenting the Best Director award, "channelled the spirit of George Jessel." Cher, on the other hand, could have used a writer—she made the embarrassing gaffe of thanking, among others, her makeup and hair people, but neither the writer who wrote her lines nor the director who helped her with them. A couple of days later she took an ad in *Variety* to rectify the omission. Oscar®-winning writer John Patrick Shanley wrote *Moonstruck* not for its Oscar®-winning star, Cher, but for another Oscar® winning star, Sally Field.

The year's great oddity was Sally Kirkland's intense campaign to get herself a nomination for *Anna* an ultra-low-budget, ultra-independent film about a Czech actress in New York. It worked, and it's no accident that even though she didn't win an Oscar®, she has ridden the publicity and the nomination—hard—ever since. Kirkland was involved with the Andy Warhol circle in the '60s, and she knew when her fifteen minutes of fame had arrived

1988

Picture	The Accidental Tourist
	Dangerous Liaisons
	Mississippi Burning
	*Rain Man
	Working Girl
Director	Charles Crichton, A Fish Called Wanda
	*Barry Levinson, Rain Man
	Mike Nichols, Working Girl
	Alan Parker, Mississippi Burning
	Martin Scorsese, The Last Temptation of Christ
Actor	Gene Hackman, Mississippi Burning
	Tom Hanks, Big
	*Dustin Hoffman, Rain Man
	Edward James Olmos, Stand and Deliver
	Max von Sydow, Pelle the Conqueror
Actress	Glenn Close, Dangerous Liaisons
	*Jodie Foster, The Accused
	Melanie Griffith, Working Girl
	Meryl Streep, A Cry in the Dark
	Sigourney Weaver, Gorillas in the Mist
Supporting Actor	Alec Guinness, Little Dorrit
	*Kevin Kline, A Fish Called Wanda
	Martin Landau, Tucker: The Man and His Dream
	River Phoenix, Running on Empty
	Dean Stockwell, Married to the Mob
Supporting Actress	Joan Cusack, Working Girl
	*Geena Davis, The Accidental Tourist
	Frances McDormand, Mississippi Burning
	Michelle Pfeiffer, Dangerous Liaisons
	Sigourney Weaver, Working Girl

Original Screenplay: Ronald Bass and Barry Morrow, *Rain Man*

Adapted Screenplay: Christopher Hampton, *Dangerous Liaisons*

Above: Barry Levinson, Best Director, *Rain Man. Right:* Tom Cruise with Best Actor Dustin Hoffman in *Rain Man.*

Foreign Film: *Pelle The Conqueror*, Denmark, Bille August

Cinematography: Peter Biziou, *Mississippi Burning*

Editing: Arthur Schmidt, *Who Framed Roger Rabbit?*

Score: Dave Grusin, *The Milagro Beanfield War*

Original Song: "Let the River Run," *Working Girl*, Carly Simon

Art Direction: Stuart Craig, *Dangerous Liaisons*

Costume Design: James Acheson, *Dangerous Liaisons*

Makeup: Ve Neill, Steve LaPorte and Robert Short, *Beetlejuice*

Visual Effects: Ken Ralston, Richard Williams, Edward Jones and George Gibbs, *Who Framed Roger Rabbit?*

Sound: Les Fresholtz, Dick Alexander, Vern Poore and Willie D. Burton, *Bird*

Sound Effects Editing: Charles L. Campbell and Louis L. Edelman, *Who Framed Roger Rabbit?*

Short films: (animated) "Tin Toy"
(live action) "The Appointments of Dennis Jennings"

Documentary: (feature) *Hotel Terminus: The Life and Times of Klaus Barbie*
(short) "You Don't Have to Die"

Thalberg Award: Not given

Jean Hersholt Humanitarian Award: Not given

Honorary Oscar®: Eastman Kodak.
The National Film Board of Canada.

Special Achievements: Richard Williams for the animation direction of *Who Framed Roger Rabbit?*

Some years after the fact, Teri Garr remarked that she hadn't thought she'd ever live down her starring role in the 1985 opening Oscar® show number. "But then there was Rob Lowe."

For some reason, producer Allan Carr, in the name of hoopla and old–fashioned showmanship, decided that the Oscars® really needed an actress garbed as Snow White, dancing furniture, waitresses in Carmen Miranda hats, and a duet between "Snow" and Rob Lowe on, of all things, "Proud Mary."

Disney sued the Academy for copyright infringement for "unauthorized and unflattering" use of the Snow White character. We were also subjected to Bruce Willis and Demi Moore's home movies of their baby, Rumer, and a musical number featuring the "stars of the future," none of whom, it seemed, were musical stars of the future.

1989

Picture	*Born on the Fourth of July* *Dead Poets Society* * *Driving Miss Daisy* *Field of Dreams* *My Left Foot*
Director	Woody Allen, *Crimes and Misdemeanors* Kenneth Branagh, *Henry V* Jim Sheridan, *My Left Foot* * Oliver Stone, *Born on the Fourth of July* Peter Weir, *Dead Poets Society*
Actor	Kenneth Branagh, *Henry V* Tom Cruise, *Born on the Fourth of July* * Daniel Day–Lewis, *My Left Foot* Morgan Freeman, *Driving Miss Daisy* Robin Williams, *Dead Poets Society*
Actress	Isabelle Adjani, *Camille Claudel* Pauline Collins, *Shirley Valentine* Jessica Lange, *The Music Box* Michelle Pfeiffer, *The Fabulous Baker Boys* * Jessica Tandy, *Driving Miss Daisy*
Supporting Actor	Danny Aiello, *Do the Right Thing* Dan Aykroyd, *Driving Miss Daisy* Marlon Brando, *A Dry White Season* Martin Landau, *Crimes and Misdemeanors* * Denzel Washington, *Glory*
Supporting Actress	* Brenda Fricker, *My Left Foot* Anjelica Huston, *Enemies, A Love Story* Lena Olin, *Enemies, A Love Story* Julia Roberts, *Steel Magnolias* Dianne Wiest, *Parenthood*

Original Screenplay: Tom Schulman, *Dead Poets Society*

Adapted Screenplay: Alfred Uhry, *Driving Miss Daisy*

Foreign Film: *Cinema Paradiso*, Italy, Giuseppe Tornatore

Cinematography: Freddie Francis, *Glory*

Left: Best Actor Daniel Day Lewis in *My Left Foot. Right:* Best Actress Jessica Tandy, with co-star Morgan Freeman, in *Driving Miss Daisy.*

Editing: David Brenner and Joe Hutshing, *Born on the Fourth of July*

Score: Alan Menken, *The Little Mermaid*

Original Song: "Under the Sea," *The Little Mermaid,* Alan Menken, music, Howard Ashman, lyrics

Art Direction: Anton Furst, *Batman*

Costume Design: Phillis Dalton, *Henry V*

Makeup: Manlio Rochetti, Lynn Barber and Kevin Haney, *Driving Miss Daisy*

Visual Effects: John Bruno, Dennis Muren, Hoyt Yeatman and Dennis Skotak, *The Abyss*

Sound: Gregg C. Rudloff, Elliott Tyson and Russell Williams II, *Glory*

Sound Effects Editing: Ben Burtt and Richard Hymns, *Indiana Jones and the Last Crusade*

Short films: (animated) "Balance"
  (live action) "Work Experience"

Documentary: (feature) *Common Threads, Stories from the Quilt*
  (short) "The Johnstown Flood"

Thalberg Award: Not given

Jean Hersholt Humanitarian Award: Howard W. Koch

Honorary Oscar®: Akira Kurosawa.

In the year of *Do the Right Thing*, Hollywood chose to honor *Driving Miss Daisy*, an uplifting film about the good old days when blacks were faithful family retainers. The Academy insulted Spike Lee when the nominations came out, with *Do the Right Thing* nominated only for screenplay and supporting actor Danny Aiello. Spike cried racism, but he should learn the Orson Welles lesson. If you keep biting Hollywood's hand, Hollywood will not pat you on the head.

Unfortunately, it was Kim Basinger who spoke out for Spike. Onstage to introduce a clip from *Dead Poets Society*, she called attention to the failure to nominate *Do the Right Thing* as an injustice. Unfortunately, because her self-designed dress was a jaw-dropping atrocity and her demeanor reflected her legendary stagefright.

Otherwise, Jessica Tandy became the oldest competitive Oscar® winner. Denzel Washington became the second black man to win supporting actor. Jane Fonda showed off new boyfriend Ted Turner and a rather impressive breast augmentation. In the wake of the lawsuits over *Coming to America* and the general revelation of how a movie which cost $20 million and grossed $200 million theatrically could still be in the red, MC Billy Crystal got the biggest laugh of the night when, following a montage celebrating "One Hundred Years of Movies," he noted that "There are 330 pieces of film in that five-minute montage and what's amazing is that, according to Paramount, not one has yet to go into profit."

Picture	*Awakenings*
	* *Dances with Wolves*
	Ghost
	The Godfather, Part III
	GoodFellas

Director	Francis Ford Coppola, *The Godfather, Part III*
	* Kevin Costner, *Dances with Wolves*
	Stephen Frears, *The Grifters*
	Barbet Schroeder, *Reversal of Fortune*
	Martin Scorsese, *GoodFellas*

Actor	Kevin Costner, *Dances with Wolves*
	Robert De Niro, *Awakenings*
	Gerard Depardieu, *Cyrano de Bergerac*
	Richard Harris, *The Field*
	* Jeremy Irons, *Reversal of Fortune*

Actress	*Kathy Bates, *Misery*
	Anjelica Huston, *The Grifters*
	Julia Roberts, *Pretty Woman*
	Meryl Streep, *Postcards from the Edge*
	Joanne Woodward, *Mr. And Mrs. Bridge*

Supporting Actor	Bruce Davison, *Longtime Companion*
	Andy Garcia, *The Godfather, Part III*
	Graham Greene, *Dances with Wolves*
	Al Pacino, *Dick Tracy*
	* Joe Pesci, *GoodFellas*

Supporting Actress	Annette Bening, *The Grifters*
	Lorraine Bracco, *GoodFellas*
	* Whoopi Goldberg, *Ghost*
	Diane Ladd, *Wild at Heart*
	Mary McDonnell, *Dances with Wolves*

Original Screenplay: Bruce Joel Rubin, *Ghost*

Adapted Screenplay: Michael Blake, *Dances with Wolves*

Foreign Film: *Journey of Hope*

Cinematography: Dean Semler, *Dances with Wolves*

Editing: Neil Travis, *Dances with Wolves*

Above: Glenn Close with Best Actor Jeremy Irons in *Reversal of Fortune*. *Right:* Kathy Bates, Best Actress, *Misery*.

Score: John Barry, *Dances with Wolves*

Original Song: "Sooner or Later (I Always Get My Man)," *Dick Tracy*, Stephen Sondheim

Art Direction: Richard Sylbert, *Dick Tracy*

Costume Design: Franca Squarciapino, *Cyrano de Bergerac*

Makeup: John Caglione, Jr. and Doug Drexler, *Dick Tracy*

Sound: Jeffrey Perkins, Bill W. Benton and Greg Watkins, *Dances with Wolves*

Sound Effects Editing: Cecelia Hall and George Watters II, *The Hunt for Red October*

283

Visual Effects: Eric Brevig, Rob Bottin, Tim McGovern and Alex Funke, *Total Recall* (Special Achievement Award)

Short films: (animated) "Creature Comforts"
(live action) "The Lunch Date"

Documentary: (feature) *American Dream*
(short) "Days of Waiting"

Thalberg Award: Richard D. Zanuck and David Brown

Jean Hersholt Humanitarian Award: Not given

Honorary Oscar®: Sophia Loren.
Myrna Loy.

Maybe Martin Scorsese shouldn't make movies in decade-starting years. In 1980, he made *Raging Bull*, got nominated as Best Director, and lost to a movie by an actor–turned–director making his first film. In 1990, he made *GoodFellas*, was nominated as Best Director, and . . . lost to Kevin Costner, whose debut won seven Oscars®, narrowly missing joining the group of elite winners with eight or more.

Whoopi Goldberg became the first black actress to win an Oscar® since Hattie McDaniel in 1939. Talk about a long time coming.

Supporting actress nominee Diane Ladd mounted the most effective campaign for a nomination: when Goldwyn Films didn't feel like spending money promoting *Wild At Heart*, Ladd got twenty cassettes of the film and offered them on loan. She had 20 Academy members over for dinner and a movie, and the movie, of course, was *Wild at Heart*.

1991

Picture	*Beauty and the Beast*
	Bugsy
	JFK
	The Prince of Tides
	* *The Silence Of The Lambs*

Director	John Singleton, *Boyz N The Hood*
	Barry Levinson, *Bugsy*
	Oliver Stone, *JFK*
	* Jonathan Demme, *The Silence Of The Lambs*
	Ridley Scott, *Thelma and Louise*

Actor	Warren Beatty, *Bugsy*
	Robert De Niro, *Cape Fear*
	* Anthony Hopkins, *The Silence Of The Lambs*
	Nick Nolte, *The Prince of Tides*
	Robin Williams, *The Fisher King*

Actress	Geena Davis, *Thelma & Louise*
	Laura Dern, *Rambling Rose*
	* Jodie Foster, *The Silence Of The Lambs*
	Bette Midler, *For the Boys*
	Susan Sarandon, *Thelma and Louise*

Supporting Actor	Tommy Lee Jones, *JFK*
	Harvey Keitel, *Bugsy*
	Ben Kingsley, *Bugsy*
	Michael Lerner, *Barton Fink*
	* Jack Palance, *City Slickers*

Supporting Actress	Diane Ladd, *Rambling Rose*
	Juliette Lewis, *Cape Fear*
	Kate Nelligan, *The Prince of Tides*
	* Mercedes Ruehl, *The Fisher King*
	Jessica Tandy, *Fried Green Tomatoes*

Original Screenplay: Callie Khouri, *Thelma and Louise*

Adapted screenplay: Ted Tally, *The Silence Of The Lambs*

Foreign Film: *Mediterraneo*, Italy, Gabriele Salvatores

Cinematography: Ralph Richardson, *JFK*

Editing: John Williams, *JFK*

Above: Best Actress Jodie Foster with Best Director Jonathan Demme, *The Silence of the Lambs.* *Right:* Best Actor Anthony Hopkins in *The Silence of the Lambs.*

Original Score: Alan Menken, *Beauty and the Beast*

Original Song: "Beauty and the Beast," *Beauty and the Beast,* music by Alan Menken, lyrics by Howard Ashman

Art Direction: *Bugsy,* Dennis Gassner

Costume Design: Albert Wolsky, *Bugsy*

Makeup: Stan Winston, Jeff Dawn, *Terminator 2*

Sound: Tom Johnson, Gary Rydstrom, Gary Summers, Lee Orloff, *Terminator 2*

Sound Effects Editing: Gary Rydstrom, Gloria S. Borders, *Terminator 2*

Short films: (animated) "Manipulation" (live action) "Session Man"

Feature Documentary: *In The Shadow of the Stars*

Documentary Short: "Deadly Deception: General Electric, Nuclear Weapons and Our Environment"

Thalberg Award: George Lucas

Honorary Oscar®: Satyajit Ray

The Silence of the Lambs, the last gasp of the slowly expiring Orion Pictures, shocked all prognosticators by becoming the first film to sweep the "big five" since *One Flew Over The Cuckoo's Nest* in 1975. In response, director Jonathan Demme gave the most incoherent acceptance speech ever made by an English speaking winner, using the word "Uh" almost forty times in a five minute speech.

The oddity of the show was Jack Palance, a surprise winner in the best supporting actor category who's acceptance speech included one–armed push–ups and provided Billy Crystal with an endless series of one–liners. The bad–hair couple of the Awards were rising star Brad Pitt and nominee Juliette Lewis *(Cape Fear)*. She demonstrated definitively why white girls should not wear cornrows.

The biggest controversy of the year arose over the documentary features category. In a year in which there had actually been documentaries that made money—*Truth Or Dare, A Brief History of Time, Hearts of Darkness: A Filmmaker's Apocalypse, 35 Up, Paris Is Burning*—the documentary nominations were a collection of unknown films. Michael Apted, director of *35 Up* and a member of the nominating committee for documentary short subjects, claimed that "the committee has an agenda. It wants to support documentaries that would not otherwise be seen. But that's not what the Academy is supposed to be about. It's supposed to be about honoring excellence. I've never heard of these films. I've never heard of these filmmakers."

1992

Picture	*The Crying Game* *A Few Good Men* *Howard's End* *Scent of a Woman* * *Unforgiven*
Director	Robert Altman, *The Player* Martin Brest, *Scent of a Woman* * Clint Eastwood, *Unforgiven* James Ivory, *Howard's End* Neil Jordan, *The Crying Game*
Actor	Robert Downey, Jr., *Chaplin* Clint Eastwood, *Unforgiven* * Al Pacino, *Scent of a Woman* Stephen Rea, *The Crying Game* Denzel Washington, *Malcolm X*
Actress	Catherine Deneuve, *Indochine* Mary McDonnell, *Passion Fish* Michelle Pfeiffer, *Love Field* Susan Sarandon, *Lorenzo's Oil* * Emma Thompson, *Howard's End*
Supporting Actor	Jaye Davidson, *The Crying Game* * Gene Hackman, *Unforgiven* Jack Nicholson, *A Few Good Men* Al Pacino, *Glengarry Glen Ross* David Paymer, *Mr. Saturday Night*
Supporting Actress	Judy Davis, *Husbands and Wives* Joan Plowright, *Enchanted April* Vanessa Redgrave, *Howard's End* Miranda Richardson, *Damage* * Marisa Tomei, *My Cousin Vinny*

Original Screenplay: Neil Jordan, *The Crying Game*

Adapted Screenplay: Ruth Prawer Jhabvala, *Howard's End*

Foreign Film: *Indochine*, France, Regis Wargnier

Cinematography: Philippe Rousselot, *A River Runs Through It*

Editing: Joel Cox, *Unforgiven*

Score: Alan Menken, *Aladdin*

Left: Best Director Clint Eastwood in Best Picture, *Unforgiven*. *Right:* Best Supporting Actress Marisa Tomei.

Original Song: "A Whole New World," *Aladdin*, Alan Menken (music), Tim Rice (lyrics)

Art Direction: Luciana Arrighi, *Howard's End*

Costume Design: Eiko Ishioka, *Bram Stoker's Dracula*

Makeup: Michele Burke, *Bram Stoker's Dracula*

Sound: Chris Jenkins, Doug Hemphill, Mark Smith, Simon Kaye, *The Last of the Mohicans*

Sound effects editing: Tom McCarthy, David Stone, *Bram Stoker's Dracula*

Short films: (animated) "Mona Lisa Descending a Staircase"

Documentary: (feature) *The Panama Deception* (short) "Education Peter"

Visual Effects: Ken Ralston, Michael Lantieri, *Death Becomes Her*

Jean Hersholt Humanitarian Award: Elizabeth Taylor for her support of AIDS research.
Audrey Hepburn (posthumously) for her work with UNICEF.

Irving Thalberg Award: Not given

Honorary Oscar®: Federico Fellini.

A subdued Oscar® ceremony, marked by tempest in a teapot controversies and what amounted to a lifetime achievement award to Clint Eastwood, as the former mayor of Carmel returned to the Awards with the first nominations of his career.

The biggest controversy came in the foreign film category. The Uruguayan nominee was judged insufficiently Uruguayan—go figure—meaning that too many of the production elements were actually Argentinian. The producers of the film pointed out that in an age of international co–production, this was hardly fair—1976's out–of–nowhere winner, *Black and White in Color*, had been listed as a production of The Ivory Coast, but most of the production personnel and cast were French.

Hollywood was much more worried about the so–called British invasion represented by *Howard's End*, *The Crying Game* and *Enchanted April*. To be fair to the Brits, the first was an Anglo–American co–production (director James Ivory is in fact an American) and the second, as writer–director Neil Jordan kept insisting to anyone who would listen at all, was an Irish film, not British at all.

The huge number of nominations to non–American films was indicative of a malaise affecting Hollywood movies in general, and the list of nominated actresses and supporting actresses made a mockery of the Oscars® celebrating "The Year of the Woman"—four of the five supporting actresses were non–Americans in non–Hollywood films, and of the five best actress nominees, only Michelle Pfeiffer and Susan Sarandon had appeared in studio films. But then, to quote Toronto film reviewer Liz Braun, "Hollywood is an irony–free zone."

Picture	*The Fugitive* *In the Name of the Father* *The Piano* *The Remains of the Day* * *Schindler's List*
Director	Jim Sheridan, *In the Name of the Father* Jane Campion, *The Piano* James Ivory, *The Remains of the Day* * Steven Spielberg, *Schindler's List* Robert Altman, *Short Cuts*
Actor	Daniel Day-Lewis, *In the Name of the Father* Laurence Fishburne, *What's Love Got to Do With It?* * Tom Hanks, *Philadelphia* Anthony Hopkins, *The Remains of the Day* Liam Neeson, *Schindler's List*
Actress	Angela Bassett, *What's Love Got to Do with It?* Stockyard Channing, *Six Degrees of Separation* * Holly Hunter, *The Piano* Emma Thompson, *The Remains of the Day* Debra Winger, *Shadowlands*
Supporting Actor	Leonardo DiCaprio, *What's Eating Gilbert Grape?* Ralph Fiennes, *Schindler's List* * Tommy Lee Jones, *The Fugitive* John Malkovich, *In the Line of Fire* Pete Postlethwaite, *In the Name of the Father*
Supporting Actress	Holly Hunter, *The Firm* * Anna Paquin, *The Piano* Rosie Perez, *Fearless* Winona Ryder, *The Age of Innocence* Emma Thompson, *In the Name of the Father*

Original Screenplay: Jane Campion, *The Piano*

Adapted Screenplay: Steve Zaillian, *Schindler's List*

Foreign Film: *Belle Epoque*, Spain

Cinematography: Janusz Kaminski, *Schindler's List*

Editing: Michael Kahn, *Schindler's List*

Left: On location in Poland, Steven Spielberg directs Liam Neeson. *Right:* Holly Hunter and Anna Paquin in *The Piano.*

Original Score: John Williams, *Schindler's List*

Original Song: "The Streets of Philadelphia," *Philadelphia,* Bruce Springsteen, music and lyrics

Art Direction: Allan Starski, Ewa Braun, *Schindler's List*

Costume Design: Gabriella Pesucci, *The Age of Innocence*

Makeup: Greg Cannom, Ve Neill, Yolanda Toussieng, *Mrs. Doubtfire*

Sound: Gary Summers, Gary Rydstrom, Shawn Murphy, Ron Judkins, *Jurassic Park*

Sound Effects Editing: Gary Rydstrom, Richard Hymns, *Jurassic Park*

Visual Effects: Dennis Muren, Stan Winston, Phil Tippett, Michael Lantieri, *Jurassic Park*

Short films: (animated) "The Wrong Trousers"
(live action) "Black Rider"

Documentary: (feature) *I Am A Promise: The Children of the Stanton Elementary School*
(short) "Defending Our Lives"

Irving Thalberg Award: Not given

Jean Hersholt Humanitarian Award: Paul Newman

Honorary Oscar®: Deborah Kerr

Hollywood movies are eligible for 18 of the 23 statuettes this year, and when the dust cleared, the score stood Steven Spielberg 10, *The Piano* 3, *Philadelphia* 2, everybody else, 3. With all the talk about the Academy members finally honoring Spielberg, about Spielberg growing up and coming to maturity with *Schindler's List*, his wins at the 1993 Academy Awards® are unprecedented. No one before has made two films which took home ten Academy Awards® in one year.

Indeed, Spielberg's victories—like Tom Hanks' for *Philadelphia* and Holly Hunter's for *The Piano*—were such a foregone conclusion that the pre-Oscar® press focused on the possibility that the anti-*Schindler*'s backlash might affect the awards. If critical backlash ever affected Hollywood, Steven Seagal wouldn't have a career. Then they worried that Whoopi Goldberg, the first woman to host the Oscars®, might say controversial or outrageous things. She didn't—her talk show demonstrated an inordinate deference to power, and her willingness to do *Sister Act II* at Disney, where she swore she'd never work again, showed that she knows which side her bread is buttered on.

Supporting actor may have been the strongest ever—John Malkovich gave a terrific performance as the villain in *In the Line of Fire,* and it was the weakest of the nominees. (Video renters seeking great acting could do far worse than the films with supporting actor nominations.) Supporting actress was one of the weirdest ever, and nobody anywhere predicted that Anna Paquin would become the second youngest acting winner ever—it was all Rosie Perez and Winona Ryder—I picked Ryder on the theory that she was the film's third lead, rather than a true supporting performance, and one could make that argument for Perez. For her part, Paquin was in shock—the sight of this little girl hyperventilating at the podium is added to the great and indelible moments in the Oscar® memory bank, to which we might also add Tom Hanks' weird, inspirational acceptance speech about his gay high school drama teacher and ending with "God Bless America."

Miscellany: Jane Campion becomes the second woman nominated as Best Director.

Best trivia question: Which living person has the most Academy Awards®? Dennis Muren, whose work as a special effects artist at Industrial Light And Magic has won him eight Oscars®. (The all time champ—Walt Disney, with 26.)

1994

Picture	*Forrest Gump
	Four Weddings and a Funeral
	Pulp Fiction
	Quiz Show
	The Shawshank Redemption

Director	Woody Allen, Bullets Over Broadway
	Krysztof Kieslowski, Red
	Robert Redford, Quiz Show
	Quentin Tarantino, Pulp Fiction
	*Robert Zemeckis, Forrest Gump

Actor	Morgan Freeman, The Shawshank Redemption
	*Tom Hanks, Forrest Gump
	Nigel Hawthorne, The Madness of King George
	Paul Newman, Nobody's Fool
	John Travolta, Pulp Fiction

Actress	Jodie Foster, Nell
	*Jessica Lange, Blue Sky
	Miranda Richardson, Tom and Viv
	Winona Ryder, Little Women
	Susan Sarandon, The Client

Supporting Actor	Samuel L. Jackson, Pulp Fiction
	*Martin Landau, Ed Wood
	Chazz Palmintieri, Bullets Over Broadway
	Paul Schofield, Quiz Show
	Gary Sinise, Forrest Gump

Supporting Actress	Rosemary Harris, Tom and Viv
	Helen Mirren, The Madness of King George
	Uma Thurman, Pulp Fiction
	Jennifer Tilly, Bullets Over Broadway
	*Dianne Wiest, Bullets Over Broadway

Original Screenplay: Quentin Tarantino and Roger Avary, *Pulp Fiction*

Adapted Screenplay: Eric Roth, *Forrest Gump*

Foreign Film: *Burnt by the Sun*, Russia, Nikita Mkhalkov

Cinematography: John Toll, *Legends of the Fall*

Editing: Arthur Schmidt, *Forrest Gump*

Original Score: Hans Zimmer, *The Lion King*

Left: Best Supporting Actress Dianne Wiest with John Cusack in *Bullets Over Broadway.*
Right: Best Actor Tom Hanks in *Forrest Gump.*

Original Song: "Can You Feel The Love Tonight," *The Lion King,* Elton John (music), Tim Rice (lyrics)

Art Direction: Ken Adam, Carolyn Scott, *The Madness of King George*

Costume Design: Lizzy Gardiner and Tim Chappel, *The Adventures of Priscilla, Queen of the Desert*

Makeup: Rick Baker, Ve Niell, Yolanda Toussieng, *Ed Wood*

Sound: Gregg Landaker, Steve Maslow, Bob Beemer, David R.B. MacMillan, *Speed*

Sound Effects Editing: Stephen Hunter Flick, *Speed*

Visual Effects: Ken Ralston, George Murphy, Stephen Rosenbaum, Allen Hall, *Forrest Gump*

Short films: (animated) "Bob's Birthday"
(live action) "Franz Kafka's It's A Wonderful Life," "Trevor," (two winners)

Documentary: (feature) *Maya Lin: A Strong Clear Vision* (short) "A Time for Justice"

Irving Thalberg Award: Clint Eastwood

Jean Hersholt Humanitarian Award: Quincy Jones

Honorary Oscar®: Michaelangelo Antonioni

1994 offered the inevitable Oscars®.

There was the annual challenge to the uselessness of the documentary nominating committee, which ignored *Hoop Dreams,* a socially important and artistically stunning three hour film documenting almost five years in the lives of two high school basketball players in Chicago.

There was the inevitable nominating problem in a major category. In one of the weakest years for actresses in recent memory, the Academy decided that Linda Fiorentino's electrifying performance in *The Last Seduction* was ineligible because the film had appeared on HBO before it appeared theatrically. The result was that Jessica Lange won for a performance in what may have been the last film to escape from the collapse of Orion, *Blue Sky*, which had been sitting on the shelf for over three years.

The biggest injustice may have been the way the Academy ignored Oliver Stone's *Natural Born Killers*, a film vastly superior to his Oscar®-winning *Born on the Fourth of July*, if you ask me.

And then there were the inevitable wins. If Las Vegas actually took bets on the Oscars® rather than merely posting the odds, the books would have taken a bath, as the favorites won in every major category. (Three of the four acting winners were getting their second Oscars®. Martin Landau was the only first-timer of the bunch.)

Let's get the inevitable Gumpism out of the way. The 1994 Oscars® were not like a box of chocolates—we knew exactly what we were going to get, and we got it. Aside from the actors, Disney won both the music categories for the fourth time in four tries. Get your money down on *Pocahontas* for '95.

Then there was the Dave controversy, as talk show host David Letterman took his first shot at hosting the show and tried to turn it into a prime time version of his own program, a debacle that provided him with months of post-Oscar® material. I thought the problem was less his material than the fact that he seemed overwhelmed by the size of the room. The Ed Sullivan Theatre is an intimate room, where he can cross the stage in about ten steps. The Dorothy Chandler Pavilion is a barn, and Letterman's brand of wiseguy sarcasm seemed to die before it crossed the footlights. Of course, the Oscars®, an evening of feigned sincerity at the best of times, are not the ideal place for someone who couldn't feign sincerity with a gun to his head.

Oddest sidelight: Whoever thought that the phrase "The Academy Award®-winning *Speed*" might be said without people giggling hysterically?

Pretty is as pretty does: Oscar®-winning costume designer Lizzy Gardiner (*The Adventures of Priscilla, Queen of the Desert*) had the evening's best outfit: a dress constructed of about 250 American Express Gold Cards. Good thing she didn't try to build a bustle, or a ball gown.

1995

Picture	*Apollo 13*
	Babe
	* *Braveheart*
	Il Postino
	Sense and Sensibility
Director	Mike Figgis, *Leaving Las Vegas*
	* Mel Gibson, *Braveheart*
	Chris Noonan, *Babe*
	Michael Radford, *Il Postino*
	Tim Robbins, *Dead Man Walking*
Actor	*Nicolas Cage, *Leaving Las Vegas*
	Richard Dreyfuss, *Mr. Holland's Opus*
	Anthony Hopkins, *Nixon*
	Sean Penn, *Dead Man Walking*
	Massimo Troisi, *Il Postino*
Actress	*Susan Sarandon, *Dead Man Walking*
	Elisabeth Shue, *Leaving Las Vegas*
	Sharon Stone, *Casino*
	Meryl Streep, *The Bridges of Madison County*
	Emma Thompson, *Sense and Sensibility*
Supporting Actor	James Cromwell, *Babe*
	Ed Harris, *Apollo 13*
	Brad Pitt, *12 Monkeys*
	Tim Roth, *Rob Roy*
	* Kevin Spacey, *The Usual Suspects*
Supporting Actress	Joan Allen, *Nixon*
	Kathleen Quinlan, *Apollo 13*
	* Mira Sorvino, *Mighty Aphrodite*
	Mare Winningham, *Georgia*
	Kate Winslet, *Sense and Sensibility*

Original Screenplay: Christopher McQuarrie, *The Usual Suspects*

Adapted Screenplay: Emma Thompson, *Sense and Sensibility*

Foreign Film: *Antonia's Line*, Netherlands, Marleen Gorris

Cinematography: John Toll, *Braveheart*

Left: Best Director, Mel Gibson, on the set of Best Picture, *Braveheart.* *Right:* Best Supporting Actress, Mira Sorvino in *Mighty Aphrodite.*

Editing: Mike Hill, Don Hanley, *Apollo 13*

Original Score: (Dramatic) Luis Bacalov, *Il Postino*
(Musical or Comedy) Alan Menken, Stephen Schwartz,
Pocahontas

Original Song: Alan Menken, Stephen Schwartz, "Colors of
the Wind," *Pocahontas*

Art Direction: Eugenio Zanetti, *Restoration*

Costume Design: James Atcheson, *Restoration*

Makeup: Peter Frampton, Paul Pattison, Lois Burwell,
Braveheart

Sound: Rick Diro, Steve Pederson, Scott Millan, David
MacMillan, *Apollo 13*

Visual Effects: Scott E. Anderson, Charles Gibson, Neal
Scanlon, John Cox, *Babe*

Sound Effects Editing: Lon Bender, Per Hallberg, *Braveheart*

Short Films: (Animated) *A Close Shave*
(Live Action) *Lieberman in Love*

Documentary: (Short) *A Survivor Remembers*
(Feature) *Anne Frank Remembered*

Honorary Oscar: Chuck Jones
Kirk Douglas

Take a close look at the Best Picture and Best Director nominations. Nineteen ninety-five was a very strange year. In a year when Hollywood made more films than usual, they couldn't find five of their own pictures to represent the best in the world.

Apollo 13 is the only traditional Hollywood studio picture in the bunch. There's the Postman from Italy, an Australian kidflick about a talking pig, an English film with a Taiwanese director and Mel Gibson's men-in-skirts epic.

Then there's the curious cases of *Leaving Las Vegas* and *Dead Man Walking*, each nominated in the director, actor, and actress categories, but not in Best Picture. *Apollo 13* and *Sense and Sensibility* are nominated (as best picture), but their directors (Ron Howard and Ang Lee) are not. To further confuse matters, the Directors Guild honors Howard as the Best Director of the year.

We are arriving at a point in Hollywood history where if one wishes to make a serious or intelligent film, one is better off working outside the system entirely. *Leaving Las Vegas* was turned down by every studio and Mike Figgis had to shoot the whole film in Super-16mm, then have it blown up to 35mm. When Susan Sarandon and Tim Robbins took *Dead Man Walking* on the rounds of the studios, they kept hearing questions like, Couldn't he turn out to be innocent? and Couldn't he escape and they could run away together? Quentin Tarantino couldn't get *Pulp Fiction* made at a studio either. Hollywood wants the hip young talents, but it doesn't actually want their films, which it seems incapable of making or marketing.

How strange a year was it? Well, it can be argued that the strongest category was Best Actress, and that hasn't happened in at least a decade. While one could protest a couple of omissions, with this year's principle victims of injustice being Jessica Lange in *Rob Roy* and Jennifer Jason Leigh in *Georgia*, it was almost impossible to suggest exactly which one of the nominees one would omit. Also, among the supporting actress nominees, Mira Sorvino was the female lead in *Mighty Aphrodite*, and Joan Allen's turn in *Nixon* was nominated in the Best Actress category at the Golden Globes.

On the subject of Best Actress nominees, Emma Thompson became the first person ever nominated as actress and for screenplay. Susan Sarandon became the first actress ever to win for playing a nun.

Odd observation: Actors won the prizes for producer and director (both Mel Gibson), adapted screenplay (Emma Thompson) and live-action short (Christine Lahti). But the Best Picture, *Braveheart*, was the only nominee in its category that had no acting nominations.

The show itself was reasonably well–done. Whoopi Goldberg returned as host and was smoking, contributing well–placed lines that actually sounded as if she had come up with them. Personal favorite: "Sharon Stone gets nominated for playing a hooker. Elisabeth Shue gets nominated for playing a hooker. Mira Sorvino gets nominated for playing a hooker. How many times did Charlie Sheen vote?"

The musical numbers weren't too embarrassing, though we could have done without the supermodel fashion show presentation of the Best Costume nominees. Robin Williams and Jim Carrey contributed hilarious bits while presenting a special Oscar® to animation legend Chuck Jones and Best Cinematography, respectively.

The most emotional moments involved parents and children. The cameras caught Best Supporting Actress Mira Sorvino's father, Paul Sorvino, weeping during his daughter's acceptance speech. She told the press later that night, "We're a very emotional family." Michael Douglas was also plainly moved when his father, Kirk, received an Honorary Award.

Best Pre–nomination campaign: Miramax took a tiny Italian film and got it five nominations, including only the fourth Best Picture nomination ever for a non–English language film. *Il Postino (The Postman)* managed nominations for Director, Actor, Screenplay, and Music.

Picture	**The English Patient* *Fargo* *Jerry Maguire* *Secrets & Lies* *Shine*
Director	Joel Coen, *Fargo* Milos Forman, *The People vs. Larry Flynt* Scott Hicks, *Shine* Mike Leigh, *Secrets & Lies* *Anthony Minghella, *The English Patient*
Actor	Tom Cruise, *Jerry Maguire* Ralph Fiennes, *The English Patient* Woody Harrelson, *The People vs. Larry Flynt* *Geoffrey Rush, *Shine* Billy Bob Thornton, *Sling Blade*
Actress	Brenda Blethyn, *Secrets & Lies* Diane Keaton, *Marvin's Room* *Frances McDormand, *Fargo* Kristin Scott Thomas, *The English Patient* Emily Watson, *Breaking the Waves*
Supporting Actor	*Cuba Gooding, Jr., *Jerry Maguire* William H. Macy, *Fargo* Armin Mueller-Stahl, *Shine* Edward Norton, *Primal Fear* James Woods, *Ghosts of Mississippi*
Supporting Actress	Joan Allen, *The Crucible* Lauren Bacall, *The Mirror Has Two Faces* *Juliette Binoche, *The English Patient* Barbara Hershey, *Portrait of a Lady* Marianne Jean-Baptiste, *Secrets & Lies*

Original Screenplay: Ethan and Joel Coen, *Fargo*

Adapted Screenplay: Billy Bob Thornton, *Sling Blade*

Foreign Film: *Kolya* (Czech Republic)

Left: David Helfgott, the adult (Geoffrey Rush), in *Shine*. *Right:* Ralph Fiennes (l) and Kristin Scott Thomas (r) in Anthony Minghella's *The English Patient*.

Cinematography: John Seale, *The English Patient*

Editing: Walter Murch, *The English Patient*

Original Score: (Dramatic) Gabriel Yared, *The English Patient* (Musical or Comedy) Rachel Portman, *Emma*

Original Song: Andrew Lloyd Webber, Tim Rice, "You Must Love Me," *Evita*

Art Direction: Stuart Craig, Stephenie McMillan, *The English Patient*

Costume Design: Ann Roth, *The English Patient*

Makeup: Rick Baker, and David Leroy Anderson, *The Nutty Professor*

Sound: Walter Murch, Mark Berger, David Parker, Chris Newman, *The English Patient*

Visual Effects: Volker Engel, Douglas Smith, Clay Pinney, Joseph Viskocil, *Independence Day*

Sound Effects Editing: Bruce Stambler, *The Ghost and the Darkness*

Short Films: (Animated) *Quest* (Live Action) *Dear Diary*

Documentary: (Feature) *When We Were Kings* (Short) *Breathing Lessons: The Life and Work of Mark O'Brien*

Honorary Oscar: Michael Kidd

Thalberg Award: Saul Zaentz

Everybody went into shock when *Jerry Maguire* turned up as the only one of the big nominees to come from a major studio, but this trend's been going on for several years. After all, when the average—that's right, the average—Hollywood studio movie costs $56 million dollars, the suits are afraid of letting the filmmakers put any brains into the picture. Twenty-five years ago, the average Hollywood movie cost $4.5 million, which today won't pay for Charlie Sheen.

The English Patient won nine Oscars®. It would have won eight, but Juliette Binoche blind-sided Lauren Bacall in the supporting actress category in what was widely perceived as a "death to Barbra Streisand" gesture.

This demonstrated the aesthetic bankruptcy of the Academy, because *The English Patient,* an almost three-hour-long love story set against the background of war, is so conventional a choice. I admit it, I didn't get this movie at all. The one good thing that I could say about *The English Patient* is that it was about an hour shorter than the actual Oscar® ceremony, which started out on the high of Billy Crystal's return as host and then Cuba Gooding, Jr.'s giddy acceptance speech, in which he used the word "love" fourteen times and then sank beneath the weight of *The English Patient*'s steamroller.

Ironically, *The English Patient* came within several inches of being a Hollywood studio production. Originally slated as a Fox production, financing fell through when director Anthony Minghella and producer Saul Zaentz refused to go along with Fox's insistence that it have a bigger star (Demi Moore) in the Kristin Scott Thomas role. Of course, had Fox produced it, it probably wouldn't have won an Oscar®, because movies starring Demi Moore don't win Oscars®. It would doubtless have had more nude scenes, though.

With the wins for *The English Patient,* Saul Zaentz, record company mogul (Fantasy) and occasional movie producer, established himself as the Sam Spiegel of our age (see entry for 1962)—a man whose films have won more Oscars® than he's made movies—*One Flew Over The Cuckoo's Nest, Amadeus,* and *The English Patient* have over 20 Oscars® between them, not bad for a producer who's made about seven films in the last 20 years. That pretty much justifies the Thalberg Award, I'd say.

1997

Picture	*As Good As It Gets*
	The Full Monty
	Good Will Hunting
	L.A. Confidential
	* *Titanic*
Actor	Matt Damon, *Good Will Hunting*
	Robert Duvall, *The Apostle*
	Peter Fonda, *Ulee's Gold*
	Dustin Hoffman, *Wag the Dog*
	*Jack Nicholson, *As Good As It Gets*
Actress	Helena Bonham Carter, *The Wings Of The Dove*
	Julie Christie, *Afterglow*
	Judi Dench, *Mrs. Brown*
	*Helen Hunt, *As Good As It Gets*
	Kate Winslet, *Titanic*
Supporting Actor	Robert Forster, *Jackie Brown*
	Anthony Hopkins, *Amistad*
	Greg Kinnear, *As Good As It Gets*
	Burt Reynolds, *Boogie Nights*
	*Robin Williams, *Good Will Hunting*
Supporting Actress	*Kim Basinger, *L.A. Confidential*
	Joan Cusack, *In & Out*
	Minnie Driver, *Good Will Hunting*
	Julianne Moore, *Boogie Nights*
	Gloria Stuart, *Titanic*
Director	Peter Cattaneo, *The Full Monty*
	Gus Van Sant, *Good Will Hunting*
	Curtis Hanson, *L.A. Confidential*
	Atom Egoyan, *The Sweet Hereafter*
	*James Cameron, *Titanic*

Foreign Film: *Character*, The Netherlands

Screenplay: Ben Affleck and Matt Damon, *Good Will Hunting*

Adapted Screenplay: Brian Helgeland and Curtis Hanson, *L.A. Confidential*

Art Direction: Peter Lamont, *Titanic*

Cinematography: Russell Carpenter, *Titanic*

Sound: Gary Rydstrom, Tom Johnson, Gary Summers, and Mark Ulano, *Titanic*

Sound Effects Editing: Tom Bellfort, Christopher Boyes, *Titanic*

Original Musical or Comedy Score: Anne Dudley, *The Full Monty*

Original Dramatic Score: James Horner, *Titanic*

Original Song: "My Heart Will Go On," *Titanic*, James Horner and Will Jennings

Costumes: Deborah L. Scott, *Titanic*

Documentary Feature: *The Long Way Home*

Documentary, Short Subject: *A Story Of Healing*

Film Editing: Conrad Buff, James Cameron, Richard A. Harris, *Titanic*

Makeup: Rick Baker, David LeRoy Anderson, *Men In Black*

Animated Short Film: *Geri's Game*

Live Action Short Film: *Visas And Virtue*

Visual Effects: Robert Legato, Mark Lasoff, Thomas L. Fisher, and Michael Kanfer, *Titanic*

Honorary Oscar: Stanley Donen

Gordon E. Sawyer Award: Don Iwerks

Scientific and Technical Award: Gunnar P. Michelson

For all the talk about the rise of the independent American cinema, *Titanic* was the fifth consecutive epic film to win Best Picture—I'm stretching a bit to include *Forrest Gump*, but it does take place over a long period of time and is set against big historical events. They'll honor small pictures—the screenplay awards to *Good Will Hunting* and *Fargo*, the occasional acting prize to the likes of Nicolas Cage and Frances MacDormand, but when it comes to the big one, size DOES matter.

With that in mind, the 70th Academy Awards® were enormous. Gigantic. Stupendous. And, at three hours and forty-six minutes, longer than *Titanic* by half an hour. They were even longer, by a minute or so, than the 1984 Oscars®. The 70th Academy Awards® Show, which began before the sun was down in Los Angeles and ended with the inevitable triumph of *Titanic*

Matt Damon and Robin Williams in *Good Will Hunting*

Helen Hunt in *As Good As It Gets*

at an hour when most decent people in James Cameron's hometown of Kapuskasing, Ontario, were in bed asleep.

It would have been one thing had there been any sort of suspense involved in the evening, but like *Titanic* itself, everyone was pretty sure how this one was going to end. (The British bookmakers had *Titanic* posted at -1000, meaning that if you wanted to bet on *Titanic* to win Best Picture you had to bet $1000 to win $100.) The question was never what would win, but only how many awards, the answer being "a lot," or eleven, more than any film since *Ben-Hur*, which, oddly enough, also managed not to win Best Screenplay.

It didn't have to be that way. The show was chugging slowly along until, at about 12:20 A.M. Eastern Time, they started the 70th Anniversary tribute to every living Oscar® winning actor, brought seventy of them up on stage, and sat them down. All over America, people were stunned into wakefulness and asking questions—mostly, "My God, is HE still alive?"

Then they finished the evening with Cameron's charmingly low-key acceptance speech, in which he had the bad taste to ask the audience in the space of a few seconds to observe a moment of silence for those who died on the *Titanic*, exhort them to party 'til dawn, and pronounce himself "King of the World."

We put forth this proposal as a cry for help: In the future, no Oscar® show can be longer than the best picture.

314

The They Don't Make 'Em Like That Anymore Award: Honorary Oscar winner Stanley Donen, director of *Singin' In The Rain* and *Funny Face* and *Pajama Game*, doing a song and dance routine. With patter!

Best dress: Minnie Driver's red Halston, which set off her scowl when her ex, Matt Damon, won his screenwriting Oscar.

Oops: Matt Damon and Ben Affleck, the noisy screenwriting winners, managed to thank lots of people in their speech. They managed to miss Kevin Smith, who directed Affleck in *Chasing Amy* and got Miramax to take a second look at their script, and their producer, Lawrence Bender.

Pre-show bad taste: Someone should tell Joan Rivers that just because Kate Winslet, smashingly curvy in green Givenchy, is not a desiccated stick insect like, say, Joan Rivers, doesn't mean that she's fat.

Most hotly debated morning-after question: Ashley Judd—was she, or wasn't she? More than one site on the Internet posted the sequence of shots of Judd walking to the podium to answer the question prompted by her slashed-to-the-hip tribute to *Basic Instinct* Richard Tyler dress. The verdict seems to be that Judd was indeed wearing underwear, but it was a close call.

1998

Picture	*Elizabeth*
	Life Is Beautiful
	*Shakespeare In Love
	Saving Private Ryan
	The Thin Red Line
Director	Roberto Benigni, *Life Is Beautiful*
	John Madden, *Shakespeare In Love*
	Terence Malick, *The Thin Red Line*
	**Steven Spielberg, *Saving Private Ryan*
	Peter Weir, *The Truman Show*
Best Actor	**Roberto Benigni, *Life Is Beautiful*
	Tom Hanks, *Saving Private Ryan*
	Ian McKellen, *Gods and Monsters*
	Nick Nolte, *Affliction*
	Edward Norton, *American History X*
Best Actress	Cate Blanchett, *Elizabeth*
	Fernanda Montenegro, *Central Station*
	**Gwynneth Paltrow, *Shakespeare In Love*
	Meryl Streep, *One True Thing*
	Emily Watson, *Hilary and Jackie*
Supporting Actor	**James Coburn, *Affliction*
	Robert Duvall, *A Civil Action*
	Ed Harris, *The Truman Show*
	Geoffrey Rush, *Shakespeare In Love*
	Billy Bob Thornton, *A Simple Plan*
Supporting Actress	Kathy Bates, *Primary Colors*
	Brenda Blethyn, *Little Voice*
	**Judi Dench, *Shakespeare In Love*
	Rachel Griffiths, *Hilary and Jackie*
	Lynn Redgrave, *Gods and Monsters*

Foreign Film: *Life Is Beautiful*, Italy

Screenplay: Marc Norman and Tom Stoppard, *Shakespeare In Love*

Adapted Screenplay: Bill Condon, *Gods and Monsters*

Art Direction: Martin Childs, *Shakespeare In Love*

Cinematography: Janusz Kaminski, *Saving Private Ryan*

Sound: Ronald Judkins, Andy Nelson, Gary Rydstrom, and Gary Summers, *Saving Private Ryan*

Sound Effects Editing: Richard Hymns and Gary Rydstrom, *Saving Private Ryan*

Original Musical or Comedy Score: Steven Warbeck, *Shakespeare In Love*

Original Dramatic Score: Nicola Piovani, *Life Is Beautiful*

Original Song: "When You Believe," Stephen Schwartz, *Prince Of Egypt*

Costumes: Sandy Powell, *Shakespeare In Love*

Editing: Michael Kahn, *Saving Private Ryan*

Makeup: Jenny Shircore, *Elizabeth*

Visual Effects: Nicholas Brooks, Joel Hynek, Kevin Mack, and Stuart Robertson, *What Dreams May Come*

Documentary Feature: *The Last Days*

Documentary Short: *The Personals: Improvisations on Romance in the Golden Years*

Live Action Short: *Election Night*

Animated Short: *Bunny*

Honorary Oscars: Elia Kazan, David Grey

Irving G. Thalberg Award: Norman Jewison

An evening to kick back, pick your favorite controversy, and enjoy. Until it clicked past the 180-minute mark with no end in sight. At the 196-minute mark—1997's record-setting running time, they were getting to the writing awards. At the start of the show, they warned us that it was going to be a long show, and they weren't kidding. Four hours of tributes, speeches, and proof that "choreographer" Debbie Allen should be collecting unemployment.

Controversy One: Should Elia Kazan be given the Lifetime Achievement Award despite the facts that he has a couple of best director Oscars® and that he named names before the House Un-American Activities Committee back in the 1950s? Blacklistees and their survivors say no. Other people say let the past bury the past. About one-third of the audience gives

Left: Gwyneth Paltrow in John Madden's *Shakespeare In Love.*
Right: Roberto Benigni in Robert Benigni's *Life Is Beautiful* (LA VITA È Bella).

Kazan a standing ovation. Some pointedly refuse to clap at all—
the cameras manage to find front-row nominees Nick Nolte
and Ed Harris among the non-clappers. Others compromise by
applauding but not standing. A damned-if-they-did-and-
damned-if-they-didn't situation. Kazan, a man with problematic
self-esteem—he's one of those very rare people who comes off
badly in his own autobiography—looked shell-shocked.

Controversy Two: How much is too much?

Did Miramax buy its Oscars® and nominations with a too big
campaign for *Shakespeare In Love*? Miramax claimed to have
spent $2 million; detractors tossed out numbers as high as $14
million.

If there was a backlash against the free-spending publicity
machine that is Miramax, it certainly didn't show up in the
voting, with Miramax picking up nine awards—seven for *Shakespeare In Love* and a pair for Roberto Benigni, the most irritat-
ing Italian export since Topo Gigio.

It's not as if Miramax's Oscar® push was a secret—it was in
all the papers, and for several weeks before the Oscars®, it was

a hot topic of discussion among people interested in the business side of the movies.

MILESTONES: Roberto Benigni becomes the first foreign-born actor in a foreign language film to win an acting prize since Sophia Loren in 1962. *Shakespeare In Love* is the first romantic comedy to win Best Picture since *Annie Hall* in 1977. Dame Judi Dench's turn in *Shakespeare In Love* is, at eight minutes, the shortest performance to win an Oscar®.

GOLDEN GIRL: Did anybody else get tired of Gwyneth Paltrow's acceptance speeches? She broke down at the Golden Globes; she broke down at the Screen Actors Guild awards. She broke down at the Oscars®. She must be fun date if you're going to a wedding. . . .

BEST PRESENTER: Jim Carrey, making hilarious comedy out of his failure to get the anticipated nomination for *The Truman Show*.

ALMOST BLUE: Clinton jokes? We all know how hard it is to get a virgin off your face? Was Whoopi Goldberg working so that she'd never be invited to host the show again?

WHAT THE HELL WAS THAT? Cowboy Heaven. Tap dancing to the music from *Life Is Beautiful*. The standard Chuck Workman clip montage—does Workman even bother anymore? Or does he just have a bin with the last shot of *City Lights* and Claudette Colbert hitchhiking and Gene Kelly hanging off the lamppost that he reaches into every year? And is it just me or did Mariah Carey and Whitney Houston not seem to be, shall we say, in full command of the lyrics of the song they were performing?

PREDICTING THE OSCARS®: WINNING YOUR OFFICE POOL

"The Golden Globes are Fun. The Oscars® are Business."
—Warren Beatty

The Office Pool

The best pool is the simplest. Every category is used, and every category is worth the same. The deductive reasoning required to figure out Best Picture and the inductive leaps for Best Short Animated film are thus worth the same.

The pool should be run by one person who will organize the forms, collect the money, and tabulate the scores. As a safety valve, this person should be required to make public his or her own picks before Oscar® night.

The next day, or at the end of the party, the winnings can be distributed. Some pools divide their winnings among the top two or three guessers. Winner–takes–all is easier however.

Complete all entries and collect all monies before the Oscar® broadcast begins. Keeping track of people's entries during the ceremony is madness, especially at a noisy party getting deeper into the wine and becoming increasingly appalled at the presenter's outfits and their inability to pronounce the names of the short film nominees.

How To Win

The difficulty in predicting who will win the Oscars® is the distance between the way we talk about "The Academy" and what it actually is.

"Historically, the Academy honors films about left-handed automechanics from Texarkana. Therefore . . ." The Academy is not a monolith. Rather, it is about 6,000 people, who are or have been employed in the film industry with some degree of regularity over a period of time. The dirty little secret of the Oscars® is that just because the voters make movies, they do not have any mystical superior insight into what makes a good film.

However, they know how much work goes into films, which accounts for the regular honoring of epic films shot in challenging locations. When a film requires a couple of hundred people to travel to Rwanda for eight months to make a three-hour movie, it's almost guaranteed to rack up some serious nominations. There is a joke that the more people a film employs, the more likely it is to get Oscar® nominations. History suggests this is more than a mere joke.

Academy members are mostly white and middle-aged, and the poorest of them are comfortably middle class. Class was the reason John Singleton's *Boyz N The Hood* was better received than Spike Lee's *Do the Right Thing*. Singleton says that the Hood needs a healthy dose of family values—in many ways, it's a Reaganite film. Lee is a stylistic anarchist and says "Fuck the police" as clearly as NWA ever did.

Unlike the Eastern critics, they are generally not suspicious of the American Dream, but see themselves as beneficiaries of it. The Academy's membership is longer on "self-made" success stories than inherited wealth. Why else did *Rocky* beat the cynically eastern *Network*, the homegrownly radical *Bound for Glory*, the anti-establishment *All the President's Men*, and the borderline psychotic *Taxi Driver* for Best Film in 1976? By any critical standards, *Rocky* is the least of those five films. But the kid from nowhere who achieves great success is a dream that many people in Hollywood believe that they have lived.

We never know how many members of the Academy vote. Several stars (Henry Fonda, for one) have been known to let their significant others fill out the ballot. Further, in the Foreign Film, Documentary, and Short categories, the voters have to see all the films—how many of the 6,000 vote for these awards?

The members of the Academy are culturally insecure. They spend their days working on *Karate Kid III* and *Kindergarten Cop*, but the face they present to the world is tuxedoed men and expensively gowned women handing statuettes to morally impeccable works that use the medium of motion pictures to illuminate the human condition.

The Oscars® are, in their way, an Aubusson rug laid over cheap, stained linoleum, a Tiffany lamp in a whorehouse. This is worth remembering when people come on and make long speeches about the nobility of their enterprise, like Sir Richard

Attenborough suggesting that honoring *Gandhi* somehow advanced the cause of world peace.

General Rules

1. Ignore your own tastes. Don't get into a lather because Barbra Streisand wasn't nominated as Best Director. Remember instead that it is rare for a film to win Best Picture and not Best Director, so it would be ill-advised to choose *The Prince of Tides* to win Best Picture. In fact, you might be better seeing none of the nominated films. In my office pool, the most successful player over the past decade is someone who rarely sees any movies at all, but simply listens to the buzz as the event itself approached.

2. Don't wait until the last minute. Around Christmas, the various critics' groups name their bests of the year. The L.A. Critics are habitually good indicators of potential winners, as is the National Board of Review. The Golden Globes are not bad, either. If your pool is big enough, it's worth working for.

On the other hand, remember Oscar®-winning screenwriter William Goldman's injunction about Hollywood. "Nobody knows anything." Think about that when you consider the improbable 1991 sweep by *The Silence of the Lambs*, which nobody predicted. On the other hand, if there is a general feeling that a film is set to sweep, pay attention. The sweeps for *Dances With Wolves*, *Gandhi*, *The Last Emperor* and *Titanic* were all predicted.

Systems are built on tendencies. But they can be wrong.

Best Picture

The longest nominated film wins Best Picture 44% of the time. The average Best Picture runs 156 minutes. Over the last decade, the average Best Picture runs 152 minutes. Only two Best Pictures ever are less than 100 minutes—*Annie Hall* and *Driving Miss Daisy*.

Comedies don't usually win Oscars®. *It Happened One Night* (1934), *You Can't Take It With You* (1938), *Going My Way* (1944), *All About Eve* (1950), *The Apartment* (1960), *Tom Jones* (1963), *The Sting* (1973), *Annie Hall* (1977). These are all the comedies which have won best picture. There are a couple of musicals which could qualify as comedies, there are movies with humor in them, but it's hard to think of a movie where a leading character dies of cancer *(Terms of Endearment)* as a comedy.

But the secret to picking best picture is in the directing Oscar®.

Best Director

Shortly before the Oscars®, the Directors' Guild announces its winner for direction of a feature film, and the DGA prize predicts who will win the best director Oscar® more than 90% of the time. This is easy information to find—most newspapers run an item in the entertainment pages.

Only four times have the Directors' Guild and the Academy disagreed on best director. Prior to 1995, when Ron Howard won the DGA for *Apollo 13* without being nominated by the Academy, the last time was in 1986, when Steven Spielberg won without receiving an Academy nomination for *The Color Purple*. This is as close to a lock as you are going to get—allowing for Howard and Spielberg, only twice since 1980 does the Directors' Guild award not predict the best picture winner. DGA = Best Director = Best Picture.

Best Screenplay

Everybody in Hollywood pays lip service to the importance of the script—"In the beginning was the word" is often heard. Between 1956 and 1994 the Best Picture winner took home a screenplay Oscar 75% of the time. Between 1979 *(Kramer vs. Kramer)* and 1994 *Forrest Gump), Platoon* was the only Best Picture winner not to take home screenplay.

While this looks like a sound system, we should observe that since *Gump* the three Best Picture winners—*Braveheart, The English Patient*, and *Titanic*, have not won best screenplay—*Titanic* wasn't even nominated.

A couple of shifts seem to have taken place.

First, screenplay is joining director as a place where the acting wing of the Academy is making its votes felt—Emma Thompson for *Sense and Sensibility*, Billy Bob Thornton for *Sling Blade*, and Matt Damon and Ben Affleck for *Good Will Hunting* make three straight wins for actors in the screenplay department. (Which seems to indicate a new trend—if someone is nominated for actor *and* screenplay, pick them to win screenplay). This has also led to the peculiar spectacle of the occasional movie with more screenwriting talent on screen than off—*Armageddon*, Disney's summer blockbuster for 1998, had a pair of Academy Award winning writers in its cast in Affleck and Thornton.

Second, where screenplay used to be a place to honor comedy films, this is now an area where the Academy is honoring independent films—all three of those mentioned, as well as *Pulp Fiction, The Usual Suspects*, and *Fargo*, fall into that category.

The best place to look for screenplay winners is still in the Best Picture category—of the past twenty screenplay awards, seventeen have gone to best picture nominees.

Acting Prizes

1. Real People: Geoffrey Rush in *Shine*, Susan Sarandon in *Dead Man Walking*, Martin Landau in *Ed Wood*, Jeremy Irons in *Reversal of Fortune*, Daniel Day-Lewis and Brenda Fricker in *My Left Foot*, F. Murray Abraham in *Amadeus*, Haing S. Ngor in *The Killing Fields*, Ben Kingsley for *Gandhi*.

2. Characters with disabilities: Geoffrey Rush in *Shine*, Al Pacino in *Scent of a Woman*, Nicolas Cage in *Leaving Las Vegas* (alcoholism), Tom Hanks in *Forrest Gump*, Daniel Day-Lewis in *My Left Foot*, Dustin Hoffman in *Rain Man*, Marlee Matlin in *Children of a Lesser God* (the fact that Matlin is actually deaf worked in her favor.) One could expand this to actors playing crazy people—Anthony Hopkins in *The Silence of the Lambs*, Kathy Bates in *Misery*, Joe Pesci in *GoodFellas*.

3. Age: Very old actors are a good bet, as are veteran actors who have never won: Al Pacino, Susan Sarandon, Jack Palance in *City Slickers*, Jessica Tandy in *Driving Miss Daisy*, Sean Connery in *The Untouchables*, Paul Newman in *The Color of Money*, Geraldine Page in *The Trip To Bountiful*, Don Ameche in *Cocoon*, Peggy Ashcroft in *A Passage to India*, Shirley MacLaine in *Terms of Endearment*, and all four 1981 acting winners—Henry Fonda and Katharine Hepburn for *On Golden Pond*, John Gielgud for *Arthur*, Maureen Stapleton for *Reds*.

4. In the supporting categories, watch out for leads nominated in support, especially for actress. Marisa Tomei is a lead in *My Cousin Vinny*. Whoopi Goldberg has leading lady screentime in *Ghost*, Geena Davis is the lead in *The Accidental Tourist*, as is Jessica Lange in *Tootsie* and Mary Steenburgen in *Melvin and Howard*. And, by the standards of Anthony Hopkins' 22-minute turn in *Silence of the Lambs*, so was Meryl Streep in *Kramer vs. Kramer*.

Also, watch for big stars in supporting roles—Sean Connery for *The Untouchables*, Michael Caine for *Hannah and Her Sisters*, Jack Nicholson in *Terms of Endearment*, Maggie Smith in *California Suite*, George Burns in *The Sunshine Boys*, Ingrid Bergman in *Murder on the Orient Express*.

5. Put your money on the Brits. In the past twenty years, 11 of the 80 acting Oscars® have gone to Brits. That includes Connery (a Scot), Hopkins (Welsh), and Peter Finch, an Australian whom everyone thought was English.

6. Accents: Hanks in *Gump*, Landau in *Ed Wood*, Tomei in *My Cousin Vinny*, Hopkins in *Silence*, Day-Lewis in *My Left Foot*, Anjelica Huston in *Prizzi's Honor*.

Actually, if we add these up, one of the most unexpected recent wins, Daniel Day-Lewis in *My Left Foot*, becomes completely predictable. He was playing a real person with an overwhelming physical handicap (author Christy Brown), and he was a British actor playing an Irishman. His chief competition that year was Tom Cruise, also playing a real person with a physical handicap, anti-war Vietnam veteran Ron Kovic. But Cruise was playing not merely an American, but someone from his own part of America, so he had no need to affect an accent.

7. Actors win for the performances they weren't honored for last year. They also win for performances they weren't nominated for this year. How much of Diane Keaton's *Annie Hall*'s win was for the serious dramatics of *Looking For Mr. Goodbar?* The year Jodie Foster won her second Oscar® for *The Silence of the Lambs*, she had also made her debut as a director. Jeremy Irons won his Oscar® the year after his highly regarded but unnominated performance in *Dead Ringers*.

Other tips: No picture has ever swept all four acting categories, not even *Gone With the Wind* (Thomas Mitchell, who played Scarlett's father in GWTW, won supporting actor for *Stagecoach*). In the past forty years—since *A Streetcar Named Desire* in 1951—only one film, *Network*, has taken three acting awards.

Foreign Film

Go figure. Some years, they pick the obvious popular film *Mediterraneo, Cinema Paradiso, The Official Story, Fanny and Alexander.* Some years they pick the film that no one's ever heard of *Journey of Hope, The Assault, Dangerous Moves, Moscow Does Not Believe in Tears.*

Foreign films do not operate under the same rules as other features. They do not have to have played theatrically, they are submitted to the Academy by their home country (one per country only, please), and screened by a nominating committee. This is a relic of the days when a foreign film had trouble opening anywhere outside New York unless it had an Academy Award®.

How do you predict the Oscar®? Carefully calculate which film is most likely to win, and pick it. Carefully calculate the film least likely to win, and pick it. Or, pick the film you've never heard of. All three systems work equally well.

Cinematography

The Academy Awards® celebrate Hollywood filmmaking but ignore American-born cameramen. Between Haskell Wexler's win for *Bound for Glory* in 1976 and Robert Richardson's 1991 win for *JFK*, no American-born cinematographer won an Oscar®. But only one truly, totally foreign language film has been honored for cinematography, when Sven Nykvist won the Oscar® for his work on Ingmar Bergman's *Fanny and Alexander*.

This trend may be in danger of disappearing, though. Three of the last four Cinematography Oscars have gone to American cinematographers—John Toll's back-to-back wins for *Legends of the Fall* and *Braveheart*, and Russell Carpenter's win for *Titanic*. Whether this is a blip in the system or a reversal of twenty years of past history remains to be seen.

The Academy has a particular fondness for the English: Freddie Francis for *Glory*, Peter Biziou for *Mississippi Burning*, Chris Menges for *The Mission* and *The Killing Fields*, David Watkin for *Out of Africa*, Billy Williams and Ronnie Taylor for *Gandhi*, Geoffrey Unsworth (and Ghislaine Cloquet) for *Tess*.

Oscar®'s favorite cinematographer is the great Italian, Vittorio Storaro, who has won for *Reds*, *The Last Emperor* and *Apocalypse Now*.

WARNING: A foreign-born cinematographer may not sound foreign. Dean Semler, for example, who won for *Dances With Wolves*, is Australian. Indeed, the closest to an American-born cinematographer to win in those years was Nestor Almendros (*Days of Heaven*, 1978) who was born ninety miles south of Florida in Cuba.

But what if there were three foreign born cinematographers nominated? Or five, as there were in 1981? The rule of thumb for cinematography, favors the outdoor over the indoor. It is considered a greater achievement to be able to photograph deserts and forests than to shoot in sets. Ridley Scott's classics, *Alien* and *Bladerunner*, were nominated for Art Direction, but not for cinematography.

Music/Song

It would be easy to recommend picking the songs Ashman and Menken did for the latest Disney Musical (*The Little Mermaid/Beauty and the Beast/Aladdin*), but Ashman died, winning his *Beauty* Oscars® posthumously. Pick the biggest hit for song, and look for picture sweeps when it comes to scores. And remember, the best or most interesting score almost never wins.

Editing/Sound/Special Effects

Since the birth of the high-tech action film, these are bones thrown to moneymakers. From *Stars Wars* to *Raiders of the Lost Ark* to *Terminator 2*.

Art Direction/Costume Design/Makeup

These awards are given less to the film with the best art direction and costume design than to the film with the most costumes and art direction. Period films and epics are always the best bet—*Room with a View, The Last Emperor, Dances With Wolves, Gandhi.*

Short Film/Animated Short/Documentary

Your guess is as good as anyone's. Films about the Nazis are popular, as are films about show business, as are films from Eastern European countries by directors with unpronounceable names.

Good luck!

Appendix—
100 Films, 100 Years

In 1998, the American Film Institute, with a nomination list of 400 films, polled 1500 people in the film industry in an effort to determine the 100 best American films.

This spawned all manner of controversy. Here is the AFI 100, with each film's Oscar wins—almost 2.5 Oscars per film. The big surprises may be that some of the films we think of as classics didn't win any Academy Awards. One third of the list—thirty-three of the films—were Best Picture winners at the Academy Awards. The highest ranking film that won no Oscars is *Singin' In The Rain*, at #10.

1. CITIZEN KANE 1941

Best Screenplay

2. CASABLANCA 1942

Best Picture
Best Director
Best Screenplay

3. THE GODFATHER 1972

Best Picture
Best Actor—Marlon Brando
Best Screenplay

4. GONE WITH THE WIND 1939

Best Picture
Best Director
Best Actress—Vivien Leigh
Best Supporting Actress—
    Hattie McDaniel
Best Screenplay
Best Cinematography
Best Editing
Best Art Direction
Thalberg Award to Selznick
Special Oscar to William
    Cameron Menzies for
    color design

5. LAWRENCE OF ARABIA 1962

Best Picture
Best Director
Best Cinematography
Best Editing
Best Score
Best Art Direction
Best Sound

6. THE WIZARD OF OZ 1939

Best Score
Best Song—"Over The
  Rainbow"

7. THE GRADUATE 1967

Best Director

8. ON THE WATERFRONT 1954

Best Picture
Best Director
Best Actor—Marlon Brando
Best Supporting Actress—
  Eva Marie Saint
Best Screenplay
Best Cinematography
Best Art Direction

9. SCHINDLER'S LIST 1993

Best Picture
Best Director
Best Screenplay
Best Cinematography
Best Editing

Best Original Score
Best Art Direction

10. SINGIN' IN THE RAIN 1952
11. IT'S A WONDERFUL LIFE 1946
12. SUNSET BOULEVARD 1950

Best Screenplay
Best Score
Best Art Direction

13. THE BRIDGE ON THE RIVER KWAI 1957

Best Picture
Best Director
Best Actor—Alec Guinness
Best Screenplay
Best Cinematography
Best Editing
Best Score

14. SOME LIKE IT HOT 1959

Best Costume Design

15. STAR WARS 1977

Best Original Score
Best Art Direction
Best Costume Design
Best Sound
Best Visual Effects

16. ALL ABOUT EVE 1950

Best Picture
Best Director

Best Supporting Actor—
  George Sanders
Best Screenplay
Best Costume Design

17. THE AFRICAN QUEEN 1951

Best Actor—Humphrey
  Bogart

18. PSYCHO 1960
19. CHINATOWN 1974

Best Screenplay

20. ONE FLEW OVER THE CUCKOO'S NEST 1975

Best Picture
Best Director
Best Actor—Jack Nicholson
Best Actress—Louise
  Fletcher
Best Screenplay

21. THE GRAPES OF WRATH 1940

Best Director
Best Supporting Actress—
  Jane Darwell

22. 2001: A SPACE ODYSSEY 1968

Visual effects

23. THE MALTESE FALCON 1941
24. RAGING BULL 1980

Best Actor—Robert De
  Niro
Best Editing

25. E.T. THE EXTRA-TERRESTRIAL 1982

Best Score
Best Sound
Best Visual Effects
Best Sound Effects Editing

26. DR. STRANGELOVE 1964
27. BONNIE AND CLYDE 1967

Best Supporting Actress—
  Estelle Parsons
Best Cinematography

28. APOCALYPSE NOW 1979

Best Cinematography
Best Sound

29. MR. SMITH GOES TO WASHINGTON 1939

Best Original Story

30. THE TREASURE OF THE SIERRA MADRE 1948

Best Director
Best Supporting Actor—

Walter Huston
Best Screenplay

31. ANNIE HALL 1977

Best Picture
Best Director
Best Actress—Diane
  Keaton
Best Screenplay

32. THE GODFATHER PART II 1974

Best Picture
Best Director
Best Supporting Actor—
  Robert DeNiro
Best Screenplay
Best Score
Best Art Direction

33. HIGH NOON 1952

Best Actor—Gary Cooper
Best Score
Best Song
Best Editing

34. TO KILL A MOCKINGBIRD 1962

Best Actor—Gregory Peck
Best Screenplay
Best Art Direction

35. IT HAPPENED ONE NIGHT 1934

Best Picture
Best Director
Best Actor—Clark Gable

Best Actress—Claudette
  Colbert
Best Screenplay

36. MIDNIGHT COWBOY 1969

Best Picture
Best Director
Best Adapted Screenplay

37. THE BEST YEARS OF OUR LIVES 1946

Best Picture
Best Director
Best Actor—Fredric March
Best Supporting Actor—
  Harold Russell
Best Screenplay
Best Original Score

38. DOUBLE INDEMNITY 1944
39. DOCTOR ZHIVAGO 1965

Adapted Screenplay
Best Cinematography
Best Original Score
Best Costume Design

40. NORTH BY NORTHWEST 1959
41. WEST SIDE STORY 1961

Best Picture
Best Director

Best Supporting Actor—
  George Chakiris
Best Supporting Actress—
  Rita Moreno
Best Cinematography
Best Editing
Best Score
Best Costume Design
Best Sound

42. REAR WINDOW 1954
43. KING KONG 1993
44. THE BIRTH OF A NATION 1915
45. A STREETCAR NAMED DESIRE 1951

Best Actress—Vivien Leigh
Best Supporting Actor—
  Karl Malden
Best Supporting Actress—
  Kim Hunter

46. A CLOCKWORK ORANGE 1971
47. TAXI DRIVER 1976
48. JAWS 1975

Best Editing
Best Original Score
Best Sound

49. SNOW WHITE AND THE SEVEN DWARFS 1937

Honorary Oscar

50. BUTCH CASSIDY AND THE SUNDANCE KID 1969

Best Screenplay

Best Cinematography
Best Original Score
Best Song

51. THE PHILADELPHIA STORY 1940

Best Actor—James Stewart

52. FROM HERE TO ETERNITY 1953

Best Picture
Best Director
Best Supporting Actor—
  Frank Sinatra
Best Supporting Actress—
  Donna Reed

53. AMADEUS 1984

Best Picture
Best Director
Best Supporting Actor—F.
  Murray Abraham
Best Screenplay
Best Art Direction
Best Costume Design

54. ALL QUIET ON THE WESTERN FRONT 1930

Best Picture
Best Director

55. THE SOUND OF MUSIC 1965

Best Picture
Best Director
Best Editing

Best Score
Best Sound

56. M*A*S*H 1970

Best Screenplay

57. THE THIRD MAN 1949
58. FANTASIA 1940
59. REBEL WITHOUT A CAUSE 1955
60. RAIDERS OF THE LOST ARK 1981

Best Editing
Best Art Direction
Best Sound
Best Visual Effects

61. VERTIGO 1958
62. TOOTSIE 1982

Best Supporting Actress—
  Jessica Lange

63. STAGECOACH 1939
64. CLOSE ENCOUNTERS OF THE THIRD KIND 1977

Best Cinematography

65. THE SILENCE OF THE LAMBS 1991

Best Picture
Best Director
Best Actor—Anthony Hopkins
Best Actress—Jodie Foster
Best Screenplay

66. NETWORK 1976

Best Actor—Peter Finch
Best Actress—Faye Dunaway
Best Supporting Actress—
  Beatrice Straight

67. THE MANCHURIAN CANDIDATE 1962
68. AN AMERICAN IN PARIS 1951

Best Picture

69. SHANE 1953
70. THE FRENCH CONNECTION 1971

Best Picture
Best Director
Best Actor—Gene Hackman

71. FORREST GUMP 1994

Best Picture
Best Director
Best Actor—Tom Hanks
Best Screenplay
Best Editing
Best Visual Effects

72. BEN-HUR 1959

Best Picture
Best Director
Best Actor—Charlton Heston
Best Supporting Actor—
  Hugh Griffith
Best Cinematography
Best Editing

Best Score
Best Art Direction
Best Costume Design
Best Sound
Best Effects

73. WUTHERING HEIGHTS 1939

Best Cinematography

74. THE GOLD RUSH 1925
75. DANCES WITH WOLVES 1990

Best Picture
Best Director
Best Screenplay
Best Cinematography
Best Editing
Best Score
Best Sound

76. CITY LIGHTS 1931
77. AMERICAN GRAFFITI 1973
78. ROCKY 1976

Best Picture
Best Director
Best Editing

79. THE DEER HUNTER 1978

Best Picture
Best Director
Best Supporting Actor—
  Christopher Walken
Best Editing
Best Sound

80. THE WILD BUNCH 1969
81. MODERN TIMES 1936
82. GIANT 1956

Best Director

83. PLATOON 1986

Best Picture
Best Director
Best Editing
Best Sound

84. FARGO 1996

Best Actress—Frances
  McDormand
Best Screenplay

85. DUCK SOUP 1933
86. MUTINY ON THE BOUNTY 1935

Best Picture

87. FRANKENSTEIN 1931
88. EASY RIDER 1969
89. PATTON 1970

Best Picture
Best Director
Best Actor—George C.
  Scott
Best Screenplay

90. THE JAZZ SINGER 1927
91. MY FAIR LADY 1964

Best Picture
Best Director

Best Actor—Rex Harrison
Best Cinematography
Best Score
Best Art Direction
Best Costume Design
Best Sound

92. A PLACE IN THE SUN 1951

93. THE APARTMENT 1960

Best Picture
Best Director
Best Screenplay

94. GOODFELLAS 1990

Best Supporting Actor—Joe Pesci

95. PULP FICTION 1994

Best Screenplay

96. THE SEARCHERS 1956

97. BRINGING UP BABY 1938

98. UNFORGIVEN 1992

Best Picture
Best Director
Best Supporting Actor—
  Gene Hackman

99. GUESS WHO'S COMING TO DINNER? 1967

Best Actress—Katherine
  Hepburn
Best Screenplay

100. YANKEE DOODLE DANDY 1942

Best Actor—James Cagney
Best Score (musical)
Best Sound

INDEX OF TITLES, DIRECTORS, AND ACTORS

341

342

348

362

363

365